MAKING SENSE OF GENESIS

MAKING SENSE OF GENESIS

Its Unfolding Ideas and Images

J. WILSON

RESOURCE *Publications* • Eugene, Oregon

MAKING SENSE OF GENESIS
Its Unfolding Ideas and Images

Copyright © 2017 J. Wilson. All rights reserved. Except for brief quotations in critical publications or reviews, no part of this book may be reproduced in any manner without prior written permission from the publisher. Write: Permissions, Wipf and Stock Publishers, 199 W. 8th Ave., Suite 3, Eugene, OR 97401.

Resource Publications
An Imprint of Wipf and Stock Publishers
199 W. 8th Ave., Suite 3
Eugene, OR 97401

www.wipfandstock.com

PAPERBACK ISBN: 978-1-4982-9076-0
HARDCOVER ISBN: 978-1-4982-9078-4
EBOOK ISBN: 978-1-4982-9077-7

Manufactured in the U.S.A.   FEBRUARY 24, 2017

Unless otherwise indicated, all Scripture quotations are from The ESV® Bible (The Holy Bible, English Standard Version®), copyright © 2001 by Crossway, a publishing ministry of Good News Publishers. Used by permission. All rights reserved.

Contents

Preface | vii
Acknowledgments | ix
List of Abbreviations | x

Chapter 1	Making Nonsense of Genesis	1
Chapter 2	The Richer Realm that Matters More	13
Chapter 3	Patterning History for a Higher Purpose	26
Chapter 4	The Unfolding Image of God	44
Chapter 5	Seed and Soil that Speak of Salvation	61
Chapter 6	Blight and Blessing in Genesis and Deuteronomy	92
Chapter 7	Ruling the Wicked and Winning the Reward	108

Bibliography | 125

Preface

AROUND THE TIME I was thinking about writing this book I was driving with one of my boys on some country back roads (in fact he was driving, hence the back roads), and I was lamenting to him that although David Byrne and his pop group *Talking Heads* had such a gift and a thoughtfulness in their music and lyrics, they hadn't won widespread affection among Australians in the way that groups like *Cold Chisel* and *Creedence* had, perhaps partly because their songs and clips weren't always easy to make sense of.

The title of this book was originally going to be *Start Making Sense*, which was adapted from one of their albums (*Stop Making Sense*). This is because the background to the book is a similar lament to the one above: that people have drifted away or turned away from God, partly because Christians and their message have stopped making sense to them, especially in our church gatherings and in our disputes. Church gatherings are often meaningless (not to mention painful and tedious) and fail to make sense of people's lives. Many people also don't understand the fights over Genesis or the emphasis on obscure details in the book of Revelation, or why churches split and won't re-unite over things like baptism and the Lord's Supper.

This in turn is partly because we've stopped making sense of our Bibles. If the different human authors of Scripture never disagree in what they write, there is a way to reach agreement about what they have said. One barrier to this is that we don't want to let go of beliefs or positions that make us feel secure in ourselves and in our church community. But obeying Jesus' call to follow him means going to him "outside the camp" as

Preface

the writer to the Hebrews puts it, and bearing "the reproach he endured."[1] This book is one fruit of my own departures from different camps, and I hope and pray that it helps the reader to hear afresh the living word of God, where Jesus calls to us and teaches us new things and old things from out of his treasury.

---

1. Hebrews 13:13.

Acknowledgments

THANKS TO WENDY FOR correcting and helping to make the manuscript more readable, to Charles and Chris for your books and feedback, to John for your last minute corrections, and to Dad, who from my earliest days faithfully testified that Genesis is true, and written by God.

List of Abbreviations

ACW	Ancient Christian Writers
BAGD	Bauer, Walter, W.F. Arndt, F.W. Gingrich, and Frederick W. Danker. *A Greek-English Lexicon of the New Testament and other Early Christian Literature*, 2nd ed. Chicago: University of Chicago Press, 1979.
BST	Bible Speaks Today
CRS	Creation Research Society
ESV	English Standard Version
JETS	Journal of the Evangelical Theological Society
LCC	Library of Christian Classics
NIV	New International Version
TOTC	Tyndale Old Testament Commentaries
Heb.	Hebrew (language)
Gen	Genesis
Exod	Exodus
Lev	Leviticus
Num	Numbers
Deut	Deuteronomy
Josh	Joshua
Judg	Judges
Sam	Samuel
Chr	Chronicles

List of Abbreviations

Ps	Psalm
Pss	Psalms
Eccl	Ecclesiastes
Isa	Isaiah
Jer	Jeremiah
Ezek	Ezekiel
Hos	Hosea
Mic	Micah
Hab	Habakkuk
Zech	Zechariah
Mal	Malachi
Matt	Matthew
Rom	Romans
Cor	Corinthians
Gal	Galatians
Eph	Ephesians
Phil	Philippians
Col	Colossians
Thess	Thessalonians
Tim	Timothy
Tit	Titus
Heb	Hebrews
Jas	James
Pet	Peter
Rev	Revelation

Chapter 1

Making Nonsense of Genesis

TROUBLE TURNING SCRIPTURE INTO SCIENCE

MOST OF MY FAVORITE books have been made into action-packed movies now, but one of the things that seem to get lost in the process is the dialogues that reveal the heart and mind of the characters who gave the stories their wide appeal. One such example is the following exchange between Sherlock Holmes and Dr Watson, who is the "I";

> "'I could hardly imagine a more damning case,' I remarked. 'If ever circumstantial evidence pointed to a criminal it does so here.'
>
> 'Circumstantial evidence is a very tricky thing,' answered Holmes thoughtfully; 'it may seem to point very straight to one thing, but if you shift your own point of view a little, you may find it pointing in an equally uncompromising manner to something entirely different.' . . . 'I am afraid,' said I, 'that the facts are so obvious that you will find little credit to be gained out of this case.'
>
> 'There is nothing more deceptive than an obvious fact,' he answered, laughing. 'Besides, we may chance to hit upon some other obvious facts which may have been by no means obvious to Mr Lestrade [a Scotland Yard detective].'"[1]

Unfortunately, my approach to interpreting Genesis has for a long time been that of the faithful Watson, which is to take it at "face value" and regard it as literal history. A key point where Holmes diverges from Watson

---

1. Conan Doyle, *Sherlock Holmes: Adventures & Memoirs*, 79.

is that he takes small details seriously, and if they cannot be made to fit the easy explanations and the big pictures, then it is the big pictures and popular reasoning that must be wrong, and Holmes sets out to discover what is really going on. This has been my own more recent journey with Genesis.

But I don't want to start with the small detail that brought my original view of Genesis unstuck, because for those who don't do biblical Hebrew it's a heavy beginning for a book. Instead, I want to prepare the scene by looking at some other problems which have become clearer since then.

One example is stellar evolution, the science of the (very slow) life cycle of stars and solar systems. It's even gaining acceptance in principle in the Creationist camp.[2] One of its conclusions is that planets form at the same time and as part of the same overall process as the birth of their governing star. A literal reading of Genesis, on the other hand, requires that the earth was formed before the sun, and that the sun was formed in a single day.

Also, Genesis 1 tells how a "firmament" or "expanse" (Heb. *raqîaʿ*) was made that separated the waters above the expanse from the waters below it, the seas.[3] The Hebrew word in question refers to something like metal that has been spread out as per Job 37:18: "Can you, like him, spread out [Heb. *tarqîaʿ*] the skies, hard as a cast metal mirror?"[4]

This understanding of the sky as a thin, impervious material rather than a void, is why Genesis views the sky as able to separate the source of rain—the "waters above the expanse"—from the seas. It's also why Genesis 1:20 describes birds as flying "*across the face of* the expanse of the heavens" (own translation) rather than "*through* the expanse of the heavens." But Genesis also says that the sun, moon, and stars are located in this "expanse."[5] Given what we now know, this would mean that the "waters above the expanse" lie on the other side of the sun, moon, and stars in outer space. So although Genesis 1 may be good at using ancient cosmology to teach about God, it falls short if we want to regard it as a cosmology in its own right.

---

2. Danny Faulkner and Don DeYoung (themselves creationists) affirm the substance of the science behind stellar evolution and regard it as a neglected area of creation science with weighty implications, in "Toward a Creationist Astronomy."

3. Genesis 1:6–10.

4. Here a different word for "skies" is used which normally means "clouds," because the writer has already used the verb for spreading out metal that the "expanse" word is derived from. If he used the "expanse" noun as well as the verb it would in Hebrew sound something like, "Can you, like him, spread the spread?"

5. Genesis 1:14, 17.

John Yeo claims that when Ancient Near Eastern science and cosmology were incorrect, the Bible only ever uses these beliefs as metaphors, in poetry but never narrative,[6] but this is not true. Another ancient misunderstanding was that beneath the earth was the void space of the underworld, and beneath this again was the subterranean freshwater sea which was called the "Abzu" by the Sumerians.[7] This subterranean sea was understood to be the source of the fresh water on the earth. This belief is reflected not only in Psalm 136:6 (among other *historical* events) but also in the Flood account, where it says that "all the fountains of the great deep burst forth" (Gen 7:11).

Another problem is how Genesis 1 portrays the discontinuity of the days in Genesis ("And there was evening, and there was morning, an Xth day"). This is alright for the first three days, where the source of light isn't specified. God could have just switched it off at night. But because Genesis 1 portrays a cosmic scale of creation rather than a local scale, and because the sun is the light source for the last three days, day is continuous at the cosmic scale from here on, because the sun doesn't switch off at night—the earth just rotates, bringing darkness to one area and day to another. So God would have been working around the clock for the last three days. Yet Genesis 1 portrays these working days of God as separated by periods of nighttime.

Also, while the NIV and ESV translate the days of creation as "the first day . . . the second day" etc., the Hebrew text reads "one day . . . a second day . . . a third day." It lacks the definiteness one would expect of a literal account of the first six days of the universe!

The location of Eden also raises problems when we try to read it literally. Eden was "in the east,"[8] meaning east of Moses' Israelite audience who were in Southern Palestine. Because a river flowed out of Eden and divided into four rivers that watered most of the known earth,[9] Eden was (or was on) a high mountain. Ezekiel shares this understanding when he says of the King of Tyre, "You were in Eden, the garden of God . . . you were on the holy mountain of God."[10]

---

6. Yeo, "Inerrancy and Historicity of Genesis."
7. Wikipedia, "Abzu."
8. Genesis 2:8.
9. Genesis 2:10–14.
10. Ezekiel 28:12–14.

But the Tigris and Euphrates (two of these four rivers that go out from Eden) converge east of Southern Palestine, at the *bottom* of their catchments. That is, the Eden of Genesis 2 indicates a geography that is entirely the reverse of the actual Tigris and Euphrates catchments. While a global flood would drastically alter geography, it's hard to imagine how it would leave these rivers in place yet reverse the tilt of the entire length of their catchments. Eden seems to belong to a different realm.[11]

Then there is the old question of how the carnivores could have been perfectly made to live on plants in the beginning as per Genesis 1:30—"To every beast of the earth and to every bird in the heavens and to everything that creeps on the earth, everything that has the breath of life, I have given every green plant for food."

It's not just a question of what some domesticated or sick carnivores will sometimes eat: it's a question of overall design and instinct. For example, the wandering albatross seems especially designed for living over and feeding from the deep ocean, so that it can sleep while flying. The changes required to make it herbivorous might leave little to distinguish it as a wandering albatross.[12]

It's not only the design of carnivores that raises questions. Herbivores are designed to live in the context of predators. For example, their eyes tend to be more protruding and located to maximize their field of vision, and their instinctive social life is built around the reality of predation. This would be odd if they were originally designed for a world with no carnivores.

Even greater problems arise when we consider the reality of ecosystems with no predators. One of the amazing things about natural ecosystems is their complexity and yet delicate balance. So when animals are introduced from outside that don't have any predators, they cause major problems very quickly, as with the historic rabbit plague in Australia and the current cane toad problem. It could be that the animals in Genesis did not have time to breed up before carnivorism came (though the text indicates otherwise if

---

11. As Gordon Wenham says, "Maybe the reversed flow of the rivers suggests that paradise is beyond man's present experience . . . maybe the insoluble geography is a way of saying that it is now inaccessible to, even unlocatable by, later man (cf. 3:24)" (Gen 1–15, 66–67).

12. Unfortunately, some Creationist speculations about how some animals became specialized carnivores after the Fall in Genesis 3, seem little different in essence to what they would call evolutionary theories. See, e.g., Wood, "Mediated Design"; Jeanson, "Did Lions Roam the Garden of Eden?", 13.

it indicates anything),[13] but Genesis 1 leaves the impression that it's talking about the natural world we live in now rather than a drastically altered one, and it concludes that it was all made well.[14] For ecosystems this requires predators to keep animal numbers in balance.

An additional problem is with the claim that there was no biological death before the Fall. The tree of life seems intended for man alone and not for the animals, so that only man was forbidden to eat from it after the Fall. Yet if man needed the tree of life to live forever, the animals would also need it as they are made from the same stuff as we are. Even in the beginning when the animals had not yet multiplied, it's hard to imagine one tree of life being enough for all of them even if it was only a small part of their diet. And if they did die, who would clean up the carcasses, with no meat-eating flies or scavengers? It's a big job for meat-eating bacteria, if they were allowed to eat meat. The beliefs that there were no biological death and no carnivores before the Fall don't seem to work.

HAGGLING OVER HEBREW GRAMMAR

But while others have turned away from a literal view of Genesis because of scientific reasons like those above, they were never enough to overturn my own view because they did not provide an alternative framework that made any better sense. For me the problem was that the chronology of creation in Genesis 1 does not match that of Genesis 2, where after God creates man in Genesis 2 he says,

> "'It is not good that the man should be alone. I will make him a helper fit for him.' And out of the ground the LORD God formed every beast of the field and every bird of the heavens. And he brought them to the man to see what he would call them." (Gen 2:18–19, own translation)

The translators of the ESV and the NIV rightly see a contradiction here with Genesis 1, where the birds and animals are made before the man.

---

13. Genesis doesn't indicate a time when carnivorism arrived among the animals, but meat was not officially granted to man till after the Flood. Also, only Adam and Eve were driven out of the garden, so Cain was born outside the garden when Adam was one hundred and thirty years old. The text doesn't indicate any significant gap in time between the Fall and the birth of Cain, in which case there would be ample time for animal numbers to explode.

14. Genesis 1:31.

Making Sense of Genesis

So the NIV and ESV translate Genesis 2:19 in the pluperfect tense—"Now out of the ground the LORD God *had formed* every beast of the field and every bird of the heavens"—as if the verse is a bracketed comment reminding us of what had happened previously.[15] But Hebrew grammar fails to support this translation, in the following way.

Hebrew narrative is normally strung together with things called *wāw*-consecutives. A *wāw*-consecutive is a Hebrew verb in a particular tense[16] with the one-letter Hebrew word *wāw* (pronounced "vāv") attached to the front of it. *Wāw* can usually be translated "And," "So," "But," "Now," or "For." Sometimes it's just a grammatical signal that doesn't need to be translated. This combination of the *wāw* attached to the verb always *begins* the sentence, as follows: "*And he formed*, the LORD God, from the ground, all the living things of the field . . . " (Gen 2:19)

The key point is that the *wāw*-consecutive is especially used for consecutive events, hence its name. The translators of the Authorized or King James Version liked to translate the *wāw* in these *wāw*-consecutives with the word "and," and one can get a good idea of how much they dominate Hebrew narrative by reading Genesis 1–2 in that version.

The normal way of including a bracketed comment would be to use a *wāw*-disjunctive, which again as its name suggests, indicates an interruption to the narrative. As well as introducing bracketed comments, the *wāw*-disjunctive is used to introduce a new subject, to sharpen contrast, or for emphasis.[17] The noun comes first instead of the verb, and has the *wāw* attached to it instead of to the verb, as follows: "*Now the earth* was formless and void . . . *Now the serpent* was more crafty than all the living things of the field . . . *Now Adam* knew his wife Eve . . . " (Gen 1:2; 3:1; 4:1)

Because the NIV and ESV translations of Genesis 2:19 involve a bracketed comment which interrupts the sequence, this would normally—some would say always—attract a *wāw*-disjunctive if this were the writer's intended meaning, rather than the *wāw*-consecutive that we find there.

But when one looks at the larger structure of the narrative the writer seems to have been very deliberate in portraying a particular sequence of events, as follows: God resolved to make a helper for the man (v 18), so he made the animals and brought them to the man who named them, but none of them were suitable helpers (vv 19–20). So God made the woman

---

15. Both the NIV and ESV put the literal reading in a footnote, however.
16. The Preterite tense.
17. Seow, *Grammar*, 149–51.

and brought her to the man (vv 21–22), and she was suitable, and he named her (v 23).

It's true that occasionally a *wāw*-consecutive can indicate the pluperfect tense, but this doesn't settle the issue because not just any pluperfect is required here. A disjunctive pluperfect is required, one that breaks the sequence of the narrative—a bracketed comment, in other words. But is the *wāw*-consecutive ever used for bracketed comments in Hebrew Scripture? The short answer is no, and those who are not into Hebrew grammar may as well jump to the next heading. The longer answer is as follows.

Waltke and O'Connor state that the *wāw*-consecutive can sometimes be "epexegetic"—that is, the event presented in the *wāw*-consecutive "does not succeed [follow] the prior one either in time or as a logical sequence; rather it explains the former situation . . . The major fact or situation is stated first, and then the particulars or details . . . are filled in"[18]—using *wāw*-consecutives. Waltke and O'Connor go on to allow the possibility of a pluperfect use as a sub-variety of the epexegetic *wāw*-consecutive, although they admit that the existence of such a use "has been controversial."[19] They give what they believe are three examples of such a use, though they omit Genesis 2:19. One of these examples is Exodus 4:19—"And the LORD said to Moses in Midian, "Go back to Egypt, for all the men who were seeking your life are dead.""

The reason some people (including the NIV but not the ESV) translate this in the pluperfect ("Now the LORD *had said* to Moses . . . ") is that they believe it refers to the previous narrative of the burning bush where the LORD first told Moses to go back to Egypt.[20] However there are several reasons for taking it as a later word to Moses when he was back with his father-in-law Jethro in Midian.

Moses associates Jethro with Midian,[21] but it's less certain that Horeb (Mt Sinai) was then regarded as part of Midian.[22] And Exodus 4:18 (the immediately preceding verse to the one in question) says, "Moses went back to Jethro his father-in-law." So the context links what God said to Moses in Exodus 4:19, with Jethro and Midian, rather than with Horeb and the burning bush. This link is strengthened by the fact that the news that those

18. Waltke & O'Connor, *Hebrew Syntax*, 551–2.
19. Ibid., 552.
20. Most firmly in Exodus 4:12.
21. Exodus 3:1.
22. Compare the comment on Exodus 4:19 by Cole, *Exodus*, 83.

who sought Moses' life were dead, was not included in the account of the burning bush at Horeb. So God seems to have given Moses a later, extra command and encouragement to go back to Egypt.

God also gives these sorts of extra commands and encouragements to Jacob when he wants him to go somewhere that might be risky—first in leaving Canaan,[23] then returning to Canaan when Esau is coming to meet him with three hundred men,[24] and finally in going down to Egypt.[25] So Exodus 4:19 is not harking back to a previous word from God: rather it records a new one. So Exodus 4:19 is not even an epexegetic *wāw*-consecutive, let alone a pluperfect.

The second example of a pluperfect that Waltke and O'Connor give, is Numbers 1:47–49: "Now the Levites were not listed along with them by their ancestral tribe, for the LORD spoke [or *had spoken*] to Moses saying, 'Only the tribe of Levi you shall not list.'" However, verse 47 begins what is a new subject in the book of Numbers—the different arrangements for the tribe of Levi—which is indicated by a *wāw*-disjunctive at the beginning of verse 47 ("*Now the Levites* were not listed"). So the *wāw*-consecutive in verse 48 is not harking back to the past for a brief moment and then returning us to the present: rather it carries forward the new material of these instructions regarding the Levites. So the ESV does not translate it in the pluperfect.

Also, the epexegetic *wāw*-consecutive is as its name suggests, epexegetical. That is, "it explains the former situation."[26] It gives the cause, the reason for it: "*For* the LORD God spoke to Moses", not "*Now* the LORD God spoke to Moses." But if such a sense were used in Genesis 2:19, it would look like this:

> "18 Then the LORD God said, 'It's not good that the man should be alone; I will make him a helper fit for him.' 19 *For* out of the ground the LORD God formed (or *had formed*) every living thing of the field."

For this to make sense, the bracketed comment would have to carry through to the end of verse 20, with pluperfect verbs all the way. This is

---

23. Genesis 28:1–2, 13–15.
24. Genesis 31:3; 32:1, 24–29.
25. Genesis 45:28—46:4.
26. Waltke & O'Connor, *Hebrew Syntax*, 552.

really stretching normal narrative structure in any language, not just Hebrew. So an epexegetic *wāw*-consecutive doesn't work in Genesis 2:19.

Waltke and O'Connor's final example of a pluperfect use of a *wāw*-consecutive, is in 1 Kings 13:12. Following is a literal translation:

> "And their father said to them, 'Which way did he go?' And his sons *had seen* the way that the man of God went, who had come from Judah."

This is indeed a pluperfect, but while it alludes to a previous event, its function in the narrative is to indicate that the sons *showed* their father the way that the man of God had taken, and both the NIV and the ESV translate it this way. That is, the *wāw*-consecutive here describes what is effectively the next event in the sequence: a consecutive event. If we knock out this event, it leaves a gap in the narrative sequence. So we could call this verb a *consecutive* pluperfect.

By contrast, the bracketed comment that some believe is the correct reading of Genesis 2:19 ("Now out of the ground the Lord God *had formed* every living thing . . . "), would be a *disjunctive* pluperfect, because it *interrupts* the narrative sequence by momentarily harking back to a previous event. So again, we would expect a *waw*-disjunctive, not the *wāw*-consecutive that we find there. So of these three examples given by Waltke and O'Connor, only one is a true pluperfect *wāw*-consecutive, and even this is not the disjunctive pluperfect that is required if we want to think that Genesis 2:19 refers to a previous event.

In addition to citing Waltke and O'Connor, Joseph Pipa lists other examples of *wāw*-consecutives which he claims are pluperfects,[27] but again they fall short of being bracketed comments. The *wāw*-consecutive in Genesis 6:12 is an epexegetic pluperfect: "*For* all flesh had corrupted their way", not "*Now* all flesh had corrupted their way." So again it functions consecutively, and doesn't work in Genesis 2:19. As in 1 Kings 13, an event expressed with a *waw*-consecutive may be chronologically prior to an event mentioned immediately before it, but it is the logical next step in the narrative.

This is the case with another of Pipa's examples: "For the famine has been in the land these two years, and there are yet five years in which there will be neither plowing nor harvest. And God *sent me* [I think this is the verb Pipa is referring to] ahead of you to preserve for you a remnant" (Gen

---

27. Pipa, "From Chaos to Cosmos."

45:6–7). This is neither an epexegetic *wāw*-consecutive ("*For* God sent me") nor a pluperfect ("God *had sent* me").

Two final texts that Pipa cites as examples of *wāw*-consecutives that are used "pluperfectly" are as follows:

> "*The* LORD *said* to Aaron, "Go into the wilderness to meet Moses." (Exod 4:27)

> "*The* LORD *said* to Moses, "Yet one plague more I will bring upon Pharaoh and upon Egypt." (Exod 11:1)

The presence of the *wāw*-consecutive is marked above by italics, but the ESV has chosen not to translate them as pluperfects (i.e., "The LORD *had* said"). Regarding Exodus 11:1, Pipa thinks that the narrative is referring back to a previous announcement about the Passover, whereas God often progressively unfolds what he will do using more than one announcement, as he did regarding his promise of offspring for Abraham. So God's announcement to Moses here is a consecutive event, not a previous one.

Regarding Exodus 4:27, it may have happened prior to verse 14 where God tells Moses that Aaron is coming out to meet him—and it may not. The Hebrew text makes no effort to clarify the question. Whether one translates this *wāw*-consecutive in the pluperfect will depend on one's confidence that it is a previous event, and on the importance one places on tidy chronology. Neither the ESV nor the NIV use an English pluperfect here. Pipa also refers to other authorities who claim that the *wāw*-consecutive sometimes loses its consecutive or sequential force, as in Jeremiah 22:15 and Ruth 2:3. However, although these examples present events that occur at the same time and are therefore not in *chronological* sequence, they are still presented in a *logical* sequence.

In summary, if we took Genesis 2:19 as a bracketed comment/disjunctive pluperfect ("Now out of the ground the Lord God *had* formed every beast . . . "), it would be a unique deviation from a norm of Hebrew grammar, and it would violate the structure of the narrative. The real driver behind this deviation is a pre-commitment to a literal reading of Genesis.

BEING NATURAL ABOUT THE SUPERNATURAL

There is a sense in which all scientists must be committed to naturalism, because the domain of science is precisely the natural world: observing and understanding natural processes and phenomena. So although Isaac Newton and Michael Faraday were believers, their vocation and goal was to understand the natural world as it is, rather than trying to accommodate it to a literal reading of Genesis. On the other hand, naturalism needs to remain open to the supernatural, and recognize its own limits. The silent question surrounding all scientific investigation is, "Where did these immaterial genetic and mathematical languages come from, that drive these natural processes?"[28]—not to mention how matter itself came to be. Problems arise when scientists begin to speculate about what they can't observe and have no empirical data for, like the origins of the human sense of the supernatural; or when scientists deny a moral order and do as they please in their research and their private lives; or when they exhaust themselves trying to find natural mechanisms for biological evolution where they may not exist.

This is the great weakness of so many evolutionary theories: they might seem right about common ancestry and the gradual arising of life, but where are the detailed pathways and feasible mechanisms for all these myriad adaptive changes to have happened without extinguishing life in the process? How did mitochondria first enter and survive and then be integrated into eukaryotic cells (the cells in multi-celled organisms)? How did the avian (bird) "flow-through" lung arise from the same ancestors that bequeathed the "in-out" lung to reptiles and mammals?[29] What is the actual pathway by which sight arose? Even "survival of the fittest" is no explanation of these mechanisms: all it does is postulate how less successful organisms were weeded out. There seems to have been a powerful and intelligent hand at work, building new creatures from old.

But it's equally fruitless to exhaust ourselves trying to come up with theories and evidence that reconcile observable and predictable natural processes with a literal reading of Genesis. Augustine of Hippo discovered this back in the fourth century. He writes:

> "Shortly after my conversion [from Manichaeism] I wrote two books against the Manichees . . . I wanted without delay either to refute their aberrations or to direct them to seek in the books

---

28. See Baumgardner & Lyon, "Linguistic Argument," 771–86.

29. In fact the avian respiratory system also includes seven or nine air sacs located around the body, and involves a sophisticated interplay of various components to achieve the necessary air pressure differential that maintains airflow. See Foster & Smith, "Respiratory System of Birds."

which they hated, the faith taught by Christ and the gospels. At that time I did not see how all of Genesis could be taken in the proper sense, and it seemed to me more and more impossible, or at least scarcely possible or very difficult, for all of it to be so understood. But not willing to be deterred from my purpose, wherever I was unable to discover the literal meaning of a passage, I explained its figurative meaning as briefly and as clearly as I was able . . . "[30]

There are several features in Augustine's thinking here that we ought to be careful of. One is an impatience to refute the thinking and convert the adherents of one's own secular background: Augustine says that he "wanted *without delay* [emphasis added] either to refute their aberrations or to direct them to seek . . . the faith."[31] Another feature is a close association between literalism and orthodoxy:[32] Augustine calls a literal sense of Genesis "the proper sense."[33] Finally, we see a new convert relying on his secular education to launch into biblical interpretation.

But Augustine was honest and humble enough to admit what we have seen in this chapter, namely that his framework for interpreting Genesis made parts of it appear nonsensical. In the next chapter we consider the Ancient Near Eastern background to Genesis, and how this can help to make more satisfying sense of it.

---

30. Hammond, *Literal Meaning of Genesis*, 1–2.

31. Ibid.

32. As with Luther's insistence on a literal interpretation of Christ's words regarding the Lord's Supper: "This is my body." See Chadwick, *Reformation*, 80.

33. Hammond, *Literal Meaning of Genesis*, 2.

Chapter 2

The Richer Realm that Matters More

LONGINGS THAT SCIENCE CAN'T SATISFY

My wife and I remember doing as all parents-to-be are instructed in Australia: sitting in the dark ultrasound room feeling chilled and invaded by both the machine and its detached operator, as she exposed the little body within to untimely human scrutiny, in grey images that meant little to us. What a contrast to the bright new life and person who arrived into our lives!

While science endeavors to reveal hidden creatures and wonders in the natural world, and to enable new pleasures and to explain our place in it all, it can have the reverse effect to the one intended. We can now look at the silver-white moon in the deep blue evening sky and know that scientific man has searched it out and found it to be a grey, dusty, lifeless waste, not really worth visiting (except for more scientific investigation). Diamonds are just carbon; the sun is a giant nuclear reaction; auroras and rainbows have their explanations; we came about by natural processes, and we will end by them when the sun moves to the "red giant" stage, if not before.[1] Commenting on the song *Sleeping Satellite* (referring to the moon), someone said "It's about the death of wonder."

Contrast this with the popularity of books like *Where the Mountain Meets the Moon*,[2] where a girl sets out on a quest (accompanied by a dragon

---

1. See also Atkinson, *Genesis 1–11*, 30.
2. Lin, *Where the Mountain Meets the Moon*.

she meets on the way) to find the Old Man of the Moon and ask him some pressing questions that affect the fortunes of her family and her friend the dragon. It's a rich story; in fact it contains many stories that each fill in a part of the main narrative. In short, to be human is to love stories and the supernatural and the magical, while science deals with explanations and the natural. We look for stories of people, their purposes, and personal causes and effects and examples, behind and above the natural processes that surround us and seem to shape our lives.

The biblical authors often share this preference for meaning-rich mythical stories. Consider the following passages—the first two about the Creation and the second two about the Exodus:

> "The pillars of heaven tremble
> and are astounded at his rebuke.
> By his power he stilled the sea;
> by his understanding he shattered Rahab.
> By his wind the heavens were made fair;
> his hand pierced the evil serpent." (Job 26:11–13, altered from ESV)

> "You rule the raging of the sea;
> when its waves rise, you still them.
> You crushed Rahab like a carcass;
> you scattered your enemies with your mighty arm." (Ps 89:9–10)

> "You divided the sea by your might;
> you broke the heads of the sea monster on the waters.
> You crushed the heads of Leviathan;
> you gave him as food for the creatures of the wilderness." (Ps 74:13–14)

> "Awake, awake, put on strength, O arm of the LORD;
> Was it not you who cut Rahab in pieces, who pierced the sea monster?
> Was it not you who dried up the sea,
> the waters of the great deep . . . ?" (Isa 51:9–10)

These stories of God subduing the seas and conquering sea monsters originate from Ancient Near Eastern myths like the *Enuma Elish* and the Baʿal cycle.[3] First the sea and then Pharaoh are symbolized as sea monsters

---

3. See Baugher, "Yahweh's Conflict"; Lam, "Biblical Creation."

The Richer Realm that Matters More

that are already familiar characters to Ancient Near Eastern readers. So these biblical authors are happy to use and adapt[4] such mythic stories in order to portray a more meaning-laden perspective on natural and human history.

So when we come to Genesis 2 we need to be wary of a literalizing perspective that irons out and surgically explains away all elements of myth and wonder, and leaves us feeling flat. To put it another way, we need to preserve the deliberate contrast between Ecclesiastes and Genesis. In Ecclesiastes 1–2 we see the world viewed from "under the sun," where there is no net gain or progress, and where even creating earthly paradise is unsatisfying. But in Genesis 1 we get to see God at work in the world, and in Genesis 2 an elusive paradise which seems to belong to a richer realm that we long for.

We saw before how Eden's geography is impossible to reconcile with the real world. Yet it's a geography that has abiding appeal: a mountain paradise with beautiful fruit trees of every kind, friendship between all animals and humankind, warm enough to walk naked in (with God!), yet with a cooling afternoon breeze,[5] and a river flowing down from and through it all. For some reason we seem to like rivers flowing down from high mountains, especially over high waterfalls: they seem as popular in art and literature now as they were in the Ancient Near East.[6]

This abiding appeal of Eden can be seen in the continued output and popularity of movies and books that involve magical realms hidden within or accessed from the observable world (as with *Harry Potter* and *Narnia*), realms that are marked by a richness and beauty that our life "under the sun" lacks. Like these realms, Eden is elusive and exclusive.

It's not the excessively fabulous realm of some modern fantasies or ancient myths, and it has a reasonable-ness and a connectedness with the real world. Yet Eden appears to satisfy our deeper longings in a way that this world and our physical appetites for it and all scientific probing into it cannot.

One of these human longings is to be royalty—to rule and somehow be closer to divine beings—and Genesis interacts with the specific expressions of that longing in Ancient Near Eastern mythology. Knowing some of this material helps us to understand how Genesis addresses this longing.

---

4. See Wenham, *Genesis* 1–15, xlviii–l.
5. Genesis 2:25; 3:8
6. See Psalm 46:4; Ezekiel 40:2; 47:1–12; Revelation 21:10; 22:1, 2.

Making Sense of Genesis

The Ancient Near Eastern stories of men who are offspring of the gods (like Adam), and who live in or travel to jewel-rich garden sanctuaries of the gods,[7] with beautiful trees and fruits irrigated by streams and rivers—these stories are usually about royal figures rather than common people. So in the Gilgamesh epic, Gilgamesh is king of Uruk and two-thirds god, one-third human.[8] In his travels towards the east (the sunrise) he comes to something on the edge of the sea that seems to be a fabulous garden or tree. It's usually understood as being a garden of the gods, although the text is incomplete at this point:[9]

> "Eleven leagues he traveled and came out before the sun (rise).
> Twelve leagues he traveled and it grew brilliant.
> . . . it bears lapis lazuli as foliage, bearing fruit, a delight to look upon.
> . . . cedar . . . agate . . . of the sea . . . lapis lazuli, like thorns and briars . . .
> . . . carnelian, rubies, hematite, . . . like . . . emeralds . . . of the sea."[10]

It's like Ezekiel's description of the king of Tyre: "You were in Eden, the garden of God; every precious stone was your covering, sardius, topaz and diamond, beryl, onyx, and jasper, sapphire, emerald and carbuncle" (Ezek 28:13).

Ezekiel makes a similar association in chapter 31 between Pharaoh and the garden of God, though the focus is on beautiful trees, especially cedars. Associating these things with royalty is understandable in the Ancient Near East, given that kings were often held to be offspring of the gods,[11] and were great builders of irrigated orchards and gardens.[12] They were also the main ones responsible for building and maintaining temples,[13] and had special access to them that was denied to most.

As we will see later on, Adam's line is indeed portrayed as a royal line in Genesis, but there is a key contrast with Ancient Near Eastern thinking

---

7. Or regular temple sanctuaries—but even these typically displayed garden themes of trees, flowers, fruit and animals, as in 1 Kings 6:18, 29; 7:18, 19, 24, 26, 29, 36.

8. Wikipedia, "Epic of Gilgamesh."

9. See synopsis of Tablet 9 in Wikipedia, "Gilgamesh"; Assyrian International News Agency, "Gilgamesh," 16; Wikipedia, "Garden of the Gods."

10. Kovacs & Carnahan, "Gilgamesh," Tablet 9.

11. E.g., Psalm 2:6, 7.

12. E.g., Solomon's irrigated parks, gardens and orchards in Ecclesiastes 1:12; 2:4–6; and the Hanging Gardens of Babylon.

13. E.g., Solomon and Herod. Regarding temple maintenance, compare Genesis 2:15 with 2 Chronicles 29:1–3; 34:8.

in that Genesis has universalized these royal privileges to all people, in a sense. That is, we are all the offspring of Adam and so of God,[14] and are all made to be kings and queens who "subdue and have dominion."[15] We are all made to live with God and have access to him,[16] and God fulfills this goal for all believers, because the kings of the earth in Revelation 21:24 who bring their glory into the city of God, represent all believers.[17] This means that the gospel—by which God completes this work of making us his royal children—must be taken to all nations.[18] It also means that we must give each person as much honor as we would give to any ruler.[19] This truth that we are made for the freedom and honor of the children of God, chimes in with our deep-seated sense of violation when we are dishonored or oppressed. But this royal identity and goal for all people is less noticeable in Genesis when we don't know the background that it was written against.[20]

MAKING MYTHIC SENSE OF THE SERPENT

Another mythic element in Eden is that it seems to have a talking snake or dragon.[21] It might be tempting for the modern reader to promptly identify it simply as Satan taking the form or possessing the body of a serpent, given the connections made in Romans 16:20 and Revelation 12:9 and 20:2. But nagging questions persist. Why, if the serpent is simply Satan in disguise, does Moses say that it was one of the creatures God had recently formed from the ground? Why, if the serpent was a real snake possessed by Satan, do all snakes apparently share in a punishment that rightly belongs to Satan alone? Why does Moses say nothing about Satan in all his inspired

---

14. Acts 17:28.

15. As the Pevensies were in the *Narnia* stories. Compare Revelation 2:26, 27; 22:5; 1 Corinthians 3:8.

16. Compare Hebrews 10:19–22; Ephesians 2:6, 11–13, 18, 22; 3:6.

17. Compare Revelation 1:6; 20:6; 22:3–4.

18. Compare Ephesians 3:6–12.

19. As in 1 Peter 2:17.

20. I have only glanced at the innumerable parallels between Genesis and other Ancient Near Eastern narratives dealing especially with creation. See, e.g., Wenham, *Genesis 1–15*, xlvii–l; Lam, "Biblical Creation," 1–5; Hewitt, "Creation Myths"; Baugher, "Yahweh's Conflict."

21. Heb. *nāḥāsh*. In Scripture it usually refers to snakes (e.g., Exod 4:3; Num 21:6) but it can refer to more dragonish and sea monster-like creatures (Isa 27:1; Job 26:13). To preserve this range of meaning it is often referred to in English versions as a serpent.

writings—which are the theological foundation of the Bible—if he has given Satan such an early debut in the serpent? Or why does Satan choose the form of a serpent (of all things) to win Eve's trust?

Or if we follow the text of Genesis and accept that the serpent was just a regular animal like the others, how was it more cunning than all the other creatures? How could it talk, and why does this pass without comment or surprise from Moses or Eve? There seems a need to widen our perspective and ask, "What is Moses interacting with and writing in the context of?"

One likely contender is the Gilgamesh epic,[22] for two reasons. One is that it contains many striking parallels with material in Genesis, as we will see below. The other is that if there has been any borrowing between the two narratives, the evidence firmly indicates that Genesis has used the Gilgamesh epic, rather than the reverse.[23]

In the epic, Gilgamesh is the pre-eminent man and king of his time. After his best friend is killed, he can't stop grieving for him or brooding on his own death. He sets off on a quest for Utnapishtim, the Mesopotamian Noah-figure who, along with his wife, has been granted immortality by the gods. When Gilgamesh comes to Utnapishtim, he tells Utnapishtim his story and asks for help to gain immortality:

> "Gilgamesh observes that Utnapishtim seems no different from himself, and asks him how he obtained his immortality. Utnapishtim explains that the gods decided to send a great Flood. To save Utnapishtim, the god Ea [the Babylonian name for the Sumerian god Enki] told him to build a boat. He gave him precise

---

22. Or the material contained therein, but originally existing separately.

23. The standard version quoted above is based on a copy that comes from the ancient library of Ashurbanipal in Nineveh, and has been dated to between 1300 and 1000 BC. But it originally existed as a set of independent Sumerian stories dating from around 2100 BC. The Old Babylonian epic form dates from around 1800–1700 BC, and the Flood narrative within the Gilgamesh epic has been copied verbatim or almost verbatim from the Atra-Hasis epic, the most complete copy of which dates to around 1650 BC (Wikipedia, "Epic of Gilgamesh"; ibid., "Atra-Hasis"). Genesis has been dated to somewhere between 1446 and 1406 BC, though many of its place names come from later times.

The key point is that while many copies and various versions and stages of the Gilgamesh and Atra-Hasis epics have been found in various ancient libraries and other sites around the Ancient Near East, no copies of or references to the book of Genesis have been found in any ancient libraries or anywhere in the Ancient Near East, in terms of time or geography. The earliest known copy of Genesis dates to no earlier than 150 BC, and was found inside Israel. So while it's easily possible that Moses and later Israelite writers were familiar with material in what is known as the standard version of the Gilgamesh epic, it's highly unlikely that many outside of Israel were familiar with Genesis.

dimensions, and it was sealed with pitch and bitumen. His entire family went aboard together with his craftsmen and "all the animals of the field". A violent storm then arose which caused the terrified gods to retreat to the heavens. Ishtar [a god] lamented the wholesale destruction of humanity, and the other gods wept beside her. The storm lasted six days and nights, after which "all the human beings turned to clay." Utnapishtim weeps when he sees the destruction. His boat lodges on a mountain, and he releases a dove, a swallow, and a raven. When the raven fails to return, he opens the ark and frees its inhabitants. Utnapishtim offers a sacrifice to the gods, who smell the sweet savor and gather around. Ishtar vows that just as she will never forget the brilliant necklace that hangs around her neck [like the rainbow in Genesis 9], she will always remember this time . . . Enlil [the supreme god in the narrative] blesses Utnapishtim and his wife, and rewards them with eternal life. This account matches the Flood story that concludes the Epic of Atrahasis."[24]

As Gilgamesh is leaving, Utnapishtim's wife asks him to offer Gilgamesh a parting gift, so Utnapishtim tells Gilgamesh about a miraculous plant that restores youth. Gilgamesh finds the plant and takes it with him, but on his way home,

> "Seeing a spring and how cool its waters were,
> Gilgamesh went down and was bathing in the water.
> A snake smelled the fragrance of the plant,
> silently came up and carried off the plant.
> While going back it sloughed off its casing [its old skin—so becoming young again]."[25]

The Gilgamesh narrative also associates wisdom with women in particular,[26] while other mythological material (notably the Atrahasis epic) especially associates wisdom with Enki, the Mesopotamian god of wisdom, craft and civilization. One compilation of ancient texts about Enki is titled *Myths of Enki, the Crafty God*.[27] And from earliest times Enki was associated (though not exclusively) with snakes.[28]

---

24. Wikipedia, "Epic of Gilgamesh", Tablet 11.
25. Kovacs & Carnahan, "Gilgamesh," Tablet 11.
26. Assyrian International News Agency, "Gilgamesh," 5.
27. Kramer & Maier, *Myths of Enki, the Crafty God*.
28. Espak, *Enki in Sumerian Royal Ideology and Mythology*, 216.

There are numerous parallels here with Genesis 1–9, but I want to focus on the role of the serpent and the woman in Genesis 3:

> "Now the serpent was more crafty than any other beast of the field that the Lord God had made. He said to the woman, 'Did God actually say, "You shall not eat of any tree in the garden?"' And the woman said to the serpent, 'We may eat of the fruit of the trees in the garden, but God said, "You shall not eat of the fruit of the tree which is in the midst of the garden, neither shall you touch it, lest you die."' But the serpent said to the woman, 'You will not surely die. For God knows that when you eat of it your eyes will be opened, and you will be like God, knowing good and evil.' So when the woman saw that the tree was good for food, and that it was a delight to the eyes, and that the tree was to be desired to make one wise, she took of its fruit and ate, and she also gave some to her husband, and he ate . . . "[29]

It's hard to deny that Moses is interacting with the material now found in the Gilgamesh and Atrahasis epics, given the currency of these narratives and ideas at the time. But this is normal for the Ancient Near East. As Peeter Espak observes, "Almost every period in Mesopotamian history introduces the re-evaluation of the pantheon and new mythological ideas. The older material is, of course, preserved in the newer thinking."[30]

And it was appropriate for Moses to interact with this "serpent" material, because;

> "Figures of bronze and stone serpents have been discovered in Canaan, Palestine, Gezer, and Transjordan, and figurines of snake goddesses, similar to those uncovered in Knossos, were unearthed in Ugarit, and in Tel Beit Mirsim in Palestine, indicating that the snake goddess was worshipped in many parts of the Ancient Near East. The tree of life was a common fixture in Near Eastern mythology and religion. It appears frequently in Babylonian and Canaanite mythology, and it was planted in the midst of the Garden of Eden (Gen. 2:9). It was also widely believed that the serpent was a symbol of rejuvenation and eternal youth . . . The veneration of the snake in the fertility cult of Canaan must have entered Europe through Minoan Crete."[31]

---

29. Genesis 3:1, 3, 4, 6, 21.
30. Espak, *Enki in Sumerian Royal Ideology and Mythology*, 238.
31. Salem & Salem, *The Near East*, 162.

So Moses had to prepare the Israelites against the religion/philosophy/culture of Canaan, which was very much associated with and symbolized by snakes.[32] It promised wisdom, but it would mean death for Israel, by causing them to violate their covenant with God.[33]

Also prominent in both Eden and the history of Israel (and a twist on the part of Utnapishtim's wife) is the role that wives can play in negatively influencing their husband's choice.[34] It's not that women are worse than men: the husbands are willing, and wives and women also help their husbands or men to make right decisions.[35] The point is rather that Abraham, Isaac, and Moses want their children (in Moses' case the children of Israel) to choose the *right* wives (as does the writer of Proverbs)[36] who will not lead them astray because they are "daughters of idolatry," and deceived as Eve was.

But the serpent in Genesis 3 is a timeless warning for us too—not to beware of talking snakes or horned devils with tails and hoofs, but to beware of and reject the purely natural and cultured wisdom which is based merely on the natural observable world, and which awakens wrong desires and finds advocates close to home who are too easy to go along with (like wives or friends). The New Testament authors rightly see that the ultimate source of man's deception is Satan, but an awareness of the Ancient Near Eastern background to the serpent in Eden provides insight into the seemingly safe quarter from which these temptations will come.

MAKING SENSE OF OUR SUBSTANCE

Man is portrayed as being formed of dust from barren ground in which nothing was yet growing. Yet our bodies break down into compost, which has a different composition to soil. And while men and women are comprised of the same stuff ("bone of my bones, and flesh of my flesh"), Genesis rightly indicates that there is a sense in which women are one step removed from the earth than men, even if they are not quite made of "sugar and

---

32. Another small way that the serpent (Hebrew *nāḥāsh*) is associated with the idolatrous practices of Canaan, is through its similarity to the Hebrew noun (*naḥash*) and verb (*nāḥash*) for divining or necromancy (Lev 19:25; Deut 18:10).
33. Deuteronomy 4:23–26; 12:29–31
34. See Genesis 3:6; 16:2–3; 24:3–4; Exodus 34:16; Deuteronomy 7:3–4; 1 Kings 11:1–8.
35. See Genesis 27:46–47; 1 Samuel 25:32–33; 2 Samuel 13:10–13; 20:16–22.
36. E.g., Proverbs 2:16–19; chapter 5; 6:23—7:27.

spice and all things nice." Men typically don't mind getting dirty so much as women, and we tend to have more to do with the earth in our work. We are rougher and less "civilized." Also, it's not logically required that man feel a bond to the woman because he's missing a rib and she is it. Rather, the narrative is a reminder and a reassurance that the woman belongs by his side: they belong together. Priority is also indicated: it's not that he belongs by *her* side as such, but that she belongs by *his*.

So Moses is helping us to understand and accept our different qualities and roles as men and women, as husband and wife. He is not telling us why or how they are so: he is rather picturing *what they are*, for the sake of harmonious and permanent marriages, among other things.

Also, because man will be made to rule over the animals (especially the land animals), he must share their substance and their social needs.[37] In this way he can have compassion on them when they are lonely and suffering—just as Jesus "had to be made like his brothers in every way," and share in our sufferings and the effects of our sins.[38]

So Genesis 2 teaches intangible truths that can't be revealed by science, and are far more important than our natural origins that science attempts to understand. Paul seems to share this perspective when he refers to the creation of the woman from the man in Genesis 2: "For man is not from woman, but woman from man."[39] Paul puts this truth in the present tense ("is", not "was"), but the NIV and ESV change it to a past tense. Paul also uses no definite articles ("man" and "woman", not "*the* man" and "*the* woman"). That is, while Paul is referring to Genesis 2, he appeals to it not as an historical event or scientific truth, but as a timeless truth of existence and relationship.

JESUS AND MOSES, THE PROPHETS OF PARABLES

Like Genesis, Jesus used familiar stories, science, and situations from the visible world to teach timeless and intangible truths. For example, the parable of the Good Samaritan has familiar echoes from real history (2 Chr 28:8–15), real life (highway robbery on the road to Jericho), and real issues (Jew–Samaritan relations). Yet it reveals the hidden ways of God.

37. Genesis 1:26–30; 2:7, 18–25.
38. Hebrews 2:17, 18.
39. 1 Corinthians 11:8.

The Richer Realm that Matters More

But while the story of the rich man and Lazarus also uses familiar figures like rich men, beggars, and Abraham, it's a little different in that it also portrays the unseen world of the afterlife. The question is whether we require Jesus' portrayal of this afterlife to be literal in the details, and consistent with what he has said elsewhere. Is it even a parable, and not a literal story? It's the last in a series of stories in Luke 15–16, the first of which is identified as a parable (Luke 15:3). All these stories begin in the same basic way:

Luke 15:4—"What man . . ." (Greek *tis anthrōpos*)
Luke 15:8—"What woman . . ." (Greek *tis gynē*)
Luke 15:11—"A certain man . . ." (Greek *anthrōpos tis*)
Luke 16:1—"A certain man . . ." (Greek *anthrōpos tis*)
Luke 16:19—"Now a certain man . . ." (Greek *anthrōpos de tis*)

So it looks like "The Rich Man and Lazarus" is a parable too, even though the editors of the NIV, the ESV, and the UBS4 Greek New Testament, don't call it a parable in contrast to the others.[40]

But is Jesus' presentation of the afterlife in this parable consistent with what he says elsewhere? Not always. For example, in the story of the sheep and the goats in Matthew 25, Jesus portrays a final judgement of everyone together, and just prior to this in the parable of the talents he speaks of an ultimate separation between the wicked and the righteous. But here in Luke 16 the rich man has received his final punishment, and Lazarus his final reward, yet the rich man's brothers haven't yet. Also, the righteous and the wicked can still see and hear and talk with each other.

So a literal portrayal of the afterlife is not Jesus' priority here, nor our business to know. He has merely used familiar figures and standard perceptions about the afterlife to say more important things that *are* our business, namely:

—prosperity in this life is not the true measure of God's blessing on righteousness

—God's punishment on the likes of the rich man is for disregarding the command Moses gave, to share his prosperity with the poor

---

40. It's possible that the editors of the NIV and ESV regarded "The Parable of the Rich Man and Lazarus" as too much of a mouthful, but then it might be better to drop "The Parable of . . " from the titles of the other parables, rather than suggest that they are less literal than "The Rich Man and Lazarus."

—Jewish disregard for Jesus is of a piece with their actual (if not perceived) disregard for Moses, in neither believing nor obeying him.

Similarly, Moses' priority in Genesis 1–2 is not a literal portrayal of the beginning, all consistent within and without. His priority—like Jesus'—is that Israel obey God and so remain in the land that he is bringing them to. Like Jesus, early Genesis uses narratives that are simple, visual, and memorable, and it uses familiar features of the observable world and stories and ideas that were familiar to Israel at the time, to teach timeless truths about God's ways and purposes. There is a genius in how Genesis can say so much that is so timeless and true in such a simple and engaging way.

So some parts of Genesis at least, seem to fit better into the category of "parable" than of "literal history" even if, like Jesus' parables, they contain historical elements from the past. Hosea at least is not afraid to associate Moses with parables:[41]

> "I spoke to the prophets; it was I who multiplied visions, and through the prophets gave parables . . . By a prophet [i.e., Moses] the LORD brought Israel up from Egypt, and by a prophet he was guarded." (Hosea 12:10, 13)

If Moses is the father of the prophets and Jesus is his particular successor,[42] and if God spoke through the prophets and especially through Jesus via parables, it leads one to expect that Moses also told parables. But where are they if they are not in Genesis? This is no proof of the parabolic nature of early Genesis, but it does make it hard to exclude the possibility.

How then do we determine which parts of Genesis are history and which are not? One way we have already been doing this is by learning about the kind of literature we are dealing with. As the apostle Paul adapted the standard letter-writing format of his time, as the wisdom writers in Israel adapted wisdom literature from Egypt and the fertile crescent, and as Moses adapted Ancient Near Eastern covenant material for Exodus and Deuteronomy, so also he adapted the Ancient Near Eastern creation and proto-historical accounts to write Genesis.

Another way we have been determining what is literal history and what is not, is by learning about the indications that God's word will often supply, just as we saw that "A certain man" means a parable is coming! In the coming chapters we will look at more indications of when Genesis is

---

41. See also Matthew 13:34–35.
42. Compare Deuteronomy 18:15–18 with John 1:21.

not literal history. But we need to be wary of pursuing this question of what is literal and what is artistic technique in Genesis, as it is too easy to become preoccupied with merely human concerns rather than any real devotion to finding out what God is saying—as it was for those who heard Jesus but didn't listen to him:

> "Where do you get that living water?" (John 4:11)

> "How can this man give us his flesh to eat?" (John 6:52)

> "How is it that you fail to understand that I did not speak about bread?" (Matt 16:1)

SQUEEZING THE JUICE OUT OF GENESIS

A literal and scientific reading of early Genesis can leave the reader feeling flat, because it flattens meaning-laden symbols into physical objects, locatable places, and subjects for scientific speculation. It flattens narratives into strict chronologies and scientific descriptions, so that we miss what they are really saying. But we long for more than this world can give, and we need more truth for really living in this world than we can find in it.[43] It's these needs that Genesis nourishes.

Part of the problem is that we are now so removed from the background that the Scriptures were written against. We don't automatically know, for example, that the book of Job is an inspired version of an established Ancient Near Eastern parable, where a righteous man suffers prolonged hardships and one or more friends counsel him with established religious doctrine.[44] Our Western eyes therefore tend to assume that it all happened exactly as set out in the book of Job—complete with a lengthy, carefully structured set of speeches. When such assumptions get challenged we can worry that God and his word are being attacked, so that we in turn attack honest brothers and sisters as Job's friends did.

---

43. As in Deuteronomy 8:3 and the conclusion of Job 28.
44. Lambert, *Babylonian Wisdom*, 63–89.

Chapter 3

Patterning History for a Higher Purpose

When my wife and I went to watch the movie *Life is Beautiful*, we weren't after a fully literal portrayal of life for a European Jewish family in the midst of World War Two. We wanted a fresh revelation of how life is indeed beautiful. While the movie was a fair enough portrayal of the period, the storyline was a bit less likely. But that was okay, because this was the vehicle for the movie's larger and truer message that love, sacrifice, and faith in providence can make life beautiful even in the midst of horror, lies, and injustice.

Matthew's gospel is a bit different in that it does indeed claim to be history. Yet Matthew's concern is more than merely a literal and chronological portrayal of Jesus' life and teaching. His eye is more on the larger picture of Jesus fulfilling all that God has said, done, and promised, hence the repeated note of fulfillment in Matthew 1–2.[1] Accordingly, Matthew doesn't mind if his readers wrongly conclude that Joseph and Mary only moved to Nazareth after Jesus was born.[2] It's more important for the Jewish Matthew that his readers see Jesus' connection with Bethlehem as the fulfillment of themes and promises from the past. The more Hellenistic[3] and scientific doctor Luke is more concerned with his audience understanding exactly when and how events actually unfolded.[4]

---

1. The more obvious ones are in Matthew 1:17, 22–23; 2:4–6, 15, 17, 23.
2. Matthew 2:22–23.
3. That is, Greek or Greek-influenced.
4. Luke 1:26–27; 2:2, 4.

There are other parts of Matthew's gospel that are even more troubling for the literal-minded Luke,[5] who doesn't seem quite satisfied with their orderliness and accuracy: "Inasmuch as many have undertaken to compile a narrative of the things that have been accomplished among us . . . it seemed good to me also, having followed all things closely for some time past, to write an orderly account for you" (Luke 1:1–3). In this chapter I hope to show that Moses is like Matthew in that he patterns his account to teach more weighty truths than mere history.

A FATHER AT WORK TO HAVE FELLOWSHIP WITH

One of the pleasures of fathers in particular, is having a little boy who wants to "come too," and feeling his little hand slip up into our own as we walk along together. One of the painful aspects for us both is when they really want to help and be involved in our work and be like us, but the task is beyond them to imitate or understand. Their desire to be like us and work with us becomes frustrated, they lose purpose, and it puts a distance between us.

The situation is similar for God and his firstborn son Israel.[6] God's purpose is to be with Israel so they can follow him, just as Jesus is Immanuel ("God with us") and he calls us to follow him. So God wants to show Israel how he works and rests, but in a way that Israel can follow him and not feel at a loose end and at a distance. But while Genesis 1 presents an example of work and rest for Israel to follow (six days of work and one of rest), God's initial creation of the primal material of the heavens and the earth out of nothing, is something that Israelites can't imitate. So some modifications are required.

One of them is that the making of the primal matter referred to in Genesis 1:1 is left outside the six days of creation, whether we take Genesis 1:1 as God's first act of creation (which the evidence firmly favors)[7] or view

---

5. Other examples include the omitted generations in Jesus' genealogy, the seeming lack of a prophecy about Jesus being called a Nazarene, and the identity of Zechariah's father in Matthew 23:35. None of these are examples of either dishonesty or error, and on meditation they invariably show Matthew's subtlety and his deep and detailed knowledge of Scripture and of God.

6. Exodus 3:22–23.

7. If Genesis 1:1 is a summary of the rest of the chapter rather than God's first act of creation, verses 2 and 7 immediately raise the question of where the earth came from. Genesis 1:1 is the obvious answer, in which case it is not a just a summary of God's

it as a summary of God's week of creation work. But a literal reading of Genesis here creates a slight discrepancy with Exodus 20:11 where God himself said to Israel, "For in six days the LORD made heaven and earth . . . and rested on the seventh day."[8]

That is, Exodus 20 seems to indicate that everything, primal matter included, was made within the six days of Genesis. One way of attempting to overcome this seeming problem is to claim that in Hebrew thinking the day begins and ends in the evening, and that this is referred to in the formula, "And there was evening, and there was morning, an Xth day." This would mean that God's creation of the primal matter of heaven and earth can be included within the "evening" of the first day.

However in Genesis 1:5 and throughout history, day is linked with light and so day did not exist before light came. This places Genesis 1:1 outside the six days of creation, and the darkness before the first day stretches back to "the beginning." Also, evening refers not to night, but to the end of the day when the light goes away. So the "evening" of verse 5 has to refer to the end of the first day, not the start of it. The formula "And there was evening etc." simply means that the previous day ended, the night was passed over without comment because no work happens at night (the norm in ancient times), and a new day came. The previous day ended with the morning of the new day. So this attempt to harmonize the chronology of Genesis and Exodus doesn't work.

The point is not that Moses has made a mistake in Genesis, but that he wants to provide an example in God that Israel can understand and imitate. There are many things God does in Genesis 1–2 that we also do in our daily work in our own way—providing light, forming things from the earth (like pottery), growing things from the earth, keeping animals and plants in their appropriate domains, speaking things and they happen (like telling someone to do something), talking to ourselves about our work, and evaluating it as good or otherwise.

Also, we see aspects of God in Genesis 1 that help our sense of closeness to him, such as his spirit literally "fluttering" like a mother bird over the

---

creative work but also a statement of his first act of creation. Also, if Genesis 1:1 were a summary of the creation account, one would expect the account to conclude by saying, "So the heavens and the earth were *created*, and all the host of them." But if Genesis 1:1 is God's first act of creation, we would expect the account to conclude as in fact it does, by saying "So the heavens and the earth were *completed*, and all the host of them" (Gen 2:1).

8. See also Exodus 31:17.

new-formed earth, God forming people with his own hands and breathing life into them, and his talking and walking with people.

But there is one aspect of God's creative work which is forever beyond us, and which therefore inspires awe rather than intimacy (as when ordinary people meet famous people), and that is God's ability to create things out of nothing. Psalm 33 points out that the natural response to this is fear and awe: "Let all the earth fear the LORD; let all the inhabitants of the world stand in awe of him! For he spoke, and it came to be; he commanded, and it stood firm" (Ps 33:8–9).

It's good and right to fear God, but his ultimate goal is to draw near to us and drive out our fear with his love, and so have us draw near to him. So although God is portrayed elsewhere as speaking the primal matter into existence, Moses passes over this here and moves promptly onto things we can relate to. This is why Moses uses the *wāw*-disjunctive at the beginning of verse 2—"*Now the earth* was shapeless and empty." It's a signal that Moses has moved onto a new subject, as it is in Genesis 3:1 and 4:1—"*Now the serpent . . . Now Adam . . .* " So the emphasis in both Exodus 20:11 and Genesis 1 is not on establishing a strict chronology of creation, but in revealing God as someone we feel a sense of fellowship with, someone we can imitate.

So we should not be surprised to learn from Jesus that God's work and rest don't actually operate according to this strict chronology of six days on and one day off: "My Father is working until now, and I am working"[9]—and this is said in reference to what Jesus had done and had instructed to be done on the Sabbath! This is why neither Christ nor any of the apostles require us to imitate God in the Sabbath regulation, which is only a shadow of God's actual work and rest.[10] As Hebrews 4 points out, the same truths still hold from Genesis, that God's rest is the true goal of his work and that while his working days have an end, his rest will be endless. But Jesus is now our example to follow, and so the New Testament writers don't even mention the six days of creation.

In fact, Hebrews 4 bases its teaching on the endlessness of God's rest partly on the fact that Genesis portrays the seventh day as endless, since it lacks the formula "And there was evening and there was morning, a seventh day."[11] So although a frequent question is "Why should we *not* understand

---

9. John 5:17.
10. Colossians 2:16, 17.
11. See Hebrews 4:3–4.

the six days as regular, twenty-four-hour days?," one answer is that Scripture itself doesn't necessarily understand the seventh day as such.

Yet the Sabbath commandment was good and righteous for Israel to keep, for several reasons. One is that bondservants had few rights and little rest in the Ancient Near East, and when Moses reiterated the Sabbath commandment in Deuteronomy he drew attention to this very fact instead of reminding Israel of God's six-day creation.[12] Also, the Sabbath required Israel to trust God to provide for them rather than relying on their own 24/7 efforts, and this would lead to Israel's holiness and blessing. Again, Moses draws attention to this in Genesis when he says that God "blessed the seventh day and made it holy, because on it he rested from all his work."[13]

In summary, there are many reasons for thinking that Moses has patterned the chronology of the creation account in Genesis for the sake of other purposes that are more important to him than literal and exact history.

WAITING FOR GOD IN THE MEANTIMES

There is another helpful and abiding truth presented in the six days of creation, namely that the times when God is evidently at work in history and in our lives, are interspersed with times when he is saying and doing nothing. Sure, God is always at work,[14] and the events that he sets in motion are always developing and ripening. But he is often also letting situations continue without intervening or explaining despite our cries:

> "We do not see our signs; there is no longer any prophet, and there is none among us who knows how long. How long, O God, is the foe to scoff? Is the enemy to revile your name forever? Why do you hold back your hand, your right hand? Take it from the fold of your garment and destroy them!" (Ps 74:9–11)

This "God of the Gaps" is a prominent feature of Genesis. Between Adam and Noah is a lengthy period with little to be said for it. After God's prophecy in Genesis 3:15–16, a period of around two thousand years is portrayed before Abraham arrives and the fulfillment gets rolling. But then it's seventy five years before God promises offspring to Abraham, and

---

12. Deuteronomy 5:14–15.
13. Genesis 2:3.
14. John 5:17.

another twenty five years before Abraham sees the first fruit of this promise in one son. Isaac and Rebekah wait twenty years for their children,[15] and Jacob has to work seven years for Rachel and then another seven.[16] Even then there is a lengthy delay before Rachel has Joseph.[17] Although Israel begins to multiply from here on, it's not until they are established in Egypt under Joseph that they really start to multiply. But again Joseph has to wait around thirteen years for the fulfillment of God's promise that his brothers will bow down to him. This includes at least two years in a foreign prison, and possibly much longer.[18]

The same pattern continues through the rest of Scripture. God is plainly beginning something new with Moses, yet another eighty years pass before he "gets the ball rolling." Then Israel wanders around in the wilderness for forty years before the conquest of Canaan. Then they are back in the spiritual doldrums while they wait for King David to come along. There is a final snapshot of these "night" times in the genealogies that span the period from the Exile to the arrival of Jesus[19]—long years with God saying and doing nothing to directly address Israel's situation. We see the same pattern in history since then: the spread of the gospel through the Roman Empire, the Reformation, the Great Awakening, the modern mission movement—and the gaps in between like the Dark Ages or (as we now call them) the Middle Ages, the night times of waiting in between.

We also see this pattern in the psalms, the prophets, and in our own lives. A frequent cry is, "How long, Lord?",[20] and a standard resolve or exhortation (or need) is to wait on God to act.[21]

While these waiting times may grow our faith and confirm that only God can save us (after we've exhausted every human option), Genesis merely wants us to understand that these gaps in between God's working days are an abiding feature of his salvation. This is a key reason for portraying creation as occurring over six days, while acknowledging the nights in between with nothing to be said for them: "And there was evening, and there was morning."

15. Genesis 25:20, 26.
16. Genesis 29:18–30.
17. Genesis 30:1–24.
18. Genesis 37:5–10; 41:1.
19. In Matthew 1 and Luke 3.
20. E.g., Psalms 13:1; 35:17; Habakkuk 1:2; Revelation 6:10.
21. E.g., Psalms 25:5; 27:14; 37:7; 123:2; Hosea 12:6.

JUDGEMENT AT THE END

So far it might be tempting to think that everyone gets a trophy from God, or that it's no problem if they don't. But there is a strong theme running through Genesis that in the end, God punishes and destroys the guilty and wicked. This theme begins with God's sentence of death on Adam, and we see a striking instance of it in the destruction of Sodom and Gomorrah.[22] But the really dominating judgement in Genesis is the Flood, where God drowned the wicked but saved righteous Noah (who found favor with God from the beginning) along with his family and a remnant of the animals.[23]

It seems more than coincidental that one of the dominating events in Israel's history is the Red Sea crossing, where God drowned Pharaoh's army and saved Israel, their livestock, and those who chose to go up with them,[24] because God had chosen Israel from long ago and Egypt was treating them wickedly.

This is just the beginning of the parallels between the Flood and the Exodus. Another is the date when both deluges began. Israel left Egypt on the fifteenth day of the second month,[25] and made their first camp at Succoth.[26] Given Israel's haste in leaving Egypt,[27] they probably headed on the next day and made their camp at Etham,[28] and their third camp on the day after (the seventeenth day of the second month) at Pi-Hahiroth.[29] During the evening, presumably of the seventeenth day of the second month, God parted the Red Sea and sometime between about 2 am and 6 am next morning, the entire Egyptian force was already within the Red Sea.[30] So they had probably begun heading into the Red Sea sometime in the night of the seventeenth day of the second month.

---

22. Also, judgement will come on the Amorites when their sin has reached its full measure (Gen 15:16); Abimelech narrowly escapes death for taking Abraham's wife (Gen 20); and two of Judah's sons are put to death for their wickedness (Gen 38:7–10).

23. Genesis 5:28–29; 6:8–9

24. Exodus 12:38.

25. Exodus 12:6, 29.

26. Exodus 12:37.

27. Exodus 12:33–34, 39.

28. Exodus 13:20.

29. Exodus 14:2.

30. Exodus 14:24.

Patterning History for a Higher Purpose

The Flood is also portrayed as beginning on the seventeenth day of the second month, in Noah's six-hundredth year.[31] The number six hundred also crops up in the Exodus: it was around six hundred thousand Israelite men who went through the Red Sea,[32] and six hundred chariots of Pharaoh that were drowned in the Red Sea.[33]

Also, at the Red Sea the Lord "drove back the sea by a strong easterly wind [Heb. *ruaḥ*]", and after the Flood he "made a wind [Heb. *ruaḥ*] blow over the earth and the waters subsided."[34] Both of these winds hark back to Genesis 1:2 where the "Spirit [Heb. *ruaḥ*] of God was fluttering over the face of the waters" (own translation) shortly before God gathered the waters under the heavens into one place, so that dry land appeared[35]—just as the Exodus wind "made the sea dry land."[36]

Then there are the parallels between their respective building works. The Flood account includes a detailed list of regulations for building the ark, along with the fact that Noah performed them all to the letter.[37] A prominent feature of Exodus is likewise a lengthy list of regulations for making the ark and tabernacle,[38] along with the repeated refrain that all of them were performed "as the Lord had commanded Moses."[39] The same basic refrain is then repeated as Moses sets it all up.[40]

There are also similarities between the dimensions of Noah's ark and the tabernacle. The ark was three hundred cubits long, and the tabernacle courtyard was three hundred cubits around. Both the tabernacle court and the ark were fifty cubits wide, and both the tabernacle and each deck of the ark were ten cubits high. These dimensions might have been fairly standard for living areas and buildings in the Ancient Near East, but it's notable that amid the large scale of the surrounding narrative in Genesis that deals with long periods and momentous events, the narrative should abruptly slow down and focus in on such minute detail that parallels the Exodus narrative.

---

31. Genesis 7:11.
32. Exodus 12:37.
33. Exodus 14:7.
34. Genesis 8:1; Exodus 14:21.
35. Genesis 1:9.
36. Exodus 14:21.
37. Genesis 6:14–22.
38. Exodus 25–30.
39. Exodus 39:1, 5, 7, 21, 26, 29, 31, 42, 43.
40. Exodus 40:16, 19, 21, 23, 25, 26, 27, 29, 32.

After Noah finished all his obedience to God he made burnt offerings of clean animals to God,[41] and when God smelled the "pleasing aroma" he resolved to overlook man's evil heart and to not curse the ground or destroy life.[42] Likewise with Moses: immediately following his obedience in setting up the tabernacle, Exodus ends, and Leviticus begins with regulations for burnt offerings of livestock which will "make atonement" for sin and be "a pleasing aroma to the LORD."[43]

So Moses seems to have shaped both the Flood account and the creation account according to what happened at the Red Sea and immediately afterwards. He is not the only biblical author who does this. John Ronning has shown how the second attack on Ai that is recorded in Joshua 8, is portrayed as a pattern of the Red Sea event.[44] Then in the book of Judges we find the following:

> "So the land had rest forty years. Then Othniel the son of Kenaz died." (Judg 3:11)

> "So Moab was subdued that day under the hand of Israel. And the land had rest for eighty years." (Judg 3:30)

> "And the land had rest for forty years." (Judg 5:31)

> "So Midian was subdued before the people of Israel, and they raised their heads no more. And the land had rest forty years in the days of Gideon." (Judg 8:28)

These verses respectively conclude the judgeships of Othniel, Ehud, Deborah and Barak, and Gideon. They point back to Noah, of whom his father Lamech said, "Out of the ground that the Lord has cursed, this one shall bring us rest."[45] But the author of Judges also seems to be looking back to Israel's forty years in the wilderness when they had a leader (Moses) who brought righteousness to Israel and therefore rest from her enemies.[46]

---

41. That is, animals that can be sacrificed according to the regulations in Leviticus.
42. Genesis 8:20–22.
43. Leviticus 1:2–4, 9, 13, 17.
44. Ronning, "When Did God Defeat Rahab/Leviathan?", 13–16.
45. Genesis 5:29.
46. Compare 2 Samuel 7:1; Jeremiah 2:2, 3.

As we have already seen, this longing for a king who will bring (God's) law and order, becomes the main focus later in the book in Judges.[47]

The point is that the author of Judges is saying more than just that each period of rest was about forty years! Granted, any such judgement of how long this "rest" lasted would be approximate, and so forty years might be a fair enough estimate, if sometimes very approximate and subjective. But the author is obviously patterning history for the sake of theology! True, theology need not exclude history, but neither Moses nor the author of Joshua and Judges (nor Matthew, as we saw earlier), are excluding history: they are merely patterning it to help us correctly interpret it. Indeed Jesus reprimands the Jews for this very failure to discern the divine pattern from the past, in what Jesus has been doing:

> "When it is evening, you say 'It will be fair weather, for the sky is red.' And in the morning, 'It will be stormy today, for the sky is red and threatening.' You know how to interpret the appearance of the sky, but you cannot interpret the signs of the times. An evil and adulterous generation seeks for a sign, but no sign shall be given to it except the sign of Jonah." (Matt 16:2–4)

That is, Jesus expected the Jews to see familiar Scriptural themes and ideas being fulfilled in what he was saying and doing and in the things that had happened and would happen to him. Yet these correspondences between Jesus and Scripture are not always obvious: not many (if any) were expecting a Messiah who would be resurrected on the third day, similar to Jonah:

> "For just as Jonah was three days and three nights in the belly of the great fish, so will the Son of Man be three days and three nights in the heart of the earth." (Matt 12:40)

So Jesus, like the biblical authors, points out these parallels for us when they don't correspond exactly: he would only be in the tomb two nights and one day, and not in what we would call the heart of the earth. It's like constellations: we look for patterns in the stars, and see familiar objects in what are often very approximate outlines. Yet there is nothing unreasonable or dishonest about this tendency that we have. We are not deterred from seeing a saucepan or a scorpion, simply because the stars don't exactly represent these objects: the starry outlines we see are close enough to be recognizable. Moses, Matthew, and Jesus are doing exactly the same thing.

---

47. Judges 18:1; 19:1; 21:25.

These patterns in history that they highlight are sufficiently evident that we *should* see them, even if there isn't exact correspondence. But just as we have to give children extra help to see the constellations, so also the biblical teachers and writers help us to see the patterns in history so we can see what God is like and have eyes opened to what he is doing now (and what he probably isn't doing that some claim he *is* doing).[48]

HOW MUCH OF GENESIS IS MYTH AND HOW MUCH DOES IT MATTER?

Different people draw the dividing line in different places in Genesis, as to where Genesis starts to become literal history. We have already seen difficulties with taking Genesis 1–3 literally, and we have seen how Moses has shaped the Flood account according to the drowning of Pharaoh's army in the Red Sea. But many people have also found pressing scientific problems with a recent global flood and re-migration of animals. One small example of the problems involved is the koala:

> "In Australia there are over 600 types of eucalypts, but koalas will only eat 40–50 varieties with only about 10 being preferred. Within a particular area, as few as one, and generally no more than two or three species of eucalypt will be regularly browsed while a variety of other species, including some non-eucalypts, appear to be browsed occasionally or used for just sitting or sleeping in ... A very slow metabolic rate allows koalas to retain food within their digestive system for a relatively long period of time, maximizing the amount of energy able to be extracted. At the same time, this slow metabolic rate minimizes energy requirements and they will sleep for up to 18 hours per day in order to conserve energy."[49]

Given the slowness of the koala, the absence of koala and *Eucalyptus* fossils on the Eurasian continent,[50] and Noah's location in or near Mesopotamia, one wonders how the koala would have fared on the journey to and from the ark, and what Noah fed it. One could come up with possible physiological or geological mechanisms that God activated during

---

48. Compare Kidner's comments on the opening verses of Psalm 78 (*Psalms 73–150*, 281).
49. Koalas: "Habitat & Diet."
50. Rozefelds, "*Eucalyptus* phylogeny and history," 19.

the Flood episode to overcome these problems, but these sorts of theories deserve the "God of the gaps" accusations they receive.[51]

Yet scientists and Ancient Near Eastern myths agree that the earth has had a very watery past. Could Moses simply write off all these "pagan myths" as having zero historical value or substance? Would it be wise for Moses to completely cut Israel off from the only accounts we know that they had of their distant past (being themselves Ancient Near Easterners)? Is this how we approach the legends of King Arthur and Sir Lancelot and Gawain? No![52] Because people of English ancestry see timeless truths in these stories, and a glimpse (uncertain though it is) into their own origins, there have been many retellings of these legends, both Christian and pagan, and much investigation into what true history they might contain. So these beloved stories are a great avenue for teaching people of English descent about the true God, and they continue to be used as such. In fact the "original" stories that we do have of King Arthur, Saint George, Beowulf, and Gawain are themselves Christian re-tellings of earlier legends that had currency at the time. Why would Moses not do the same with Ancient Near Eastern literary works, that had such currency with Israel that later psalmists were still using them, as we saw with Psalm 74?

Even the later New Testament writers are happy to use non-historical and non-Scriptural literature where it suits their pastoral purposes, has currency with their audience, and contains figures and events from their own past that form a part of their own identity. Peter Davids has shown that the letters of James, Jude, and Peter frequently cite the examples of Old Testament figures, not from the Old Testament itself, but from later Jewish apocryphal works. One instance of this is James' use of the example of Job:

> "When it comes to Job, the discussion in James revolves around *hypomonē* [a Greek word meaning patient endurance] in both its nominal [noun] and verbal forms. The problem is that neither the verb nor the noun appears in the LXX[53] of Job. Nor would one necessarily attribute this virtue to the Job of canonical Job[54] (cf., e.g., Job 7:11-16; 10:18; 23:3; 30:20-23). This Job does not curse

---

51. I.e., God has supernatural power that can fix up any scientific dilemmas with a literal reading of Genesis. See, e.g., Matson, "Young-Earth Arguments?", para. 21.

52. Nor do believers make haste to dismiss the entirety of the accounts of early martyrs such as Polycarp and evangelists such as Patrick, even when they contain some rather suspicious parts.

53. A Greek translation of the Old Testament.

54. I.e., the Job in the biblical book of Job.

> God, but he certainly argues loudly that God has made a mistake. Faithful he is, but patient endurance does not come to mind in reading the text. All this changes, however, when one reads the *Testament of Job*,[55] for the whole work revolves around *hypomonē* . . . Gone are Job's complaints . . . Through it all Job remains so patient that he will not even let a maggot drop prematurely from its burrow in his skin . . . This is the reading of the Job narrative that makes sense of James's reference."[56]

So for Peter, James, and Jude the issue was not whether the sources they used were historically reliable, or even claimed to be history. The issue was whether these stories held forth the non-literal truths that they wanted their audiences to approve and practice, and whether they had currency with their audience as did the *Testament of Job*, since James writes, "*You have heard* of the patient endurance of Job" (own translation).[57]

The more literal-minded among us might still appreciate having some way of knowing which parts of Genesis are literal history, and if we can draw a dividing line somewhere, say between chapters 1–11 and chapters 12–50. To help understand whether we can do this or not, I want to compare the Genesis account of Joseph with the Gilgamesh epic (which as we have already seen, seems to have existed earlier and much more widely than Genesis), to see if there is any evidence that Moses has used material from the Gilgamesh epic to fill out his narrative of Joseph. Following are extracts from both accounts, and then a list of similarities between them:

> "Now Joseph was handsome in form and appearance. And after a time his master's wife cast her eyes on Joseph and said, 'Lie with me.' But he refused . . . But one day, when he went into the house to do his work and none of the men of the house was there in the house, she caught him by his garment, saying, 'Lie with me.' But he left his garment in her hand and fled and got out of the house. And as soon as she saw that he had left his garment in her hand and had fled out of the house, she called to the men of her household and said to them, 'See, he has brought among us a Hebrew to laugh at us. He came in to me to lie with me, and I cried out with a loud voice. And as soon as he heard that I lifted up my voice and cried out, he left his garment beside me and fled and got out of the house.' Then she laid up his garment by her until his master came

---

55. A Jewish apocryphal work.
56. Davids, "What Glasses are you Wearing?", 765.
57. James 5:11.

home, and she told him the same story, saying, 'The Hebrew servant, whom you have brought among us, came in to me to laugh at me. But as soon as I lifted up my voice and cried, he left his garment beside me and fled out of the house.'

" . . . Then Pharaoh sent and called Joseph, and they quickly brought him out of the pit. And when he had shaved himself and changed his clothes, he came in before Pharaoh . . . Then Joseph said to Pharaoh, ' . . . The seven lean and ugly cows that came up after them, and the seven empty ears blighted by the east wind, are also seven years of famine. It is as I told Pharaoh; God has shown to Pharaoh what he is about to do. There will come seven years of great plenty throughout all the land of Egypt, but after them there will arise seven years of famine, and all the plenty will be forgotten . . . Now therefore let Pharaoh select a discerning and wise man, and set him over the land of Egypt. Let Pharaoh proceed to appoint overseers over the land and take one-fifth of the produce of the land of Egypt during the seven plentiful years. And let them gather all the food of these good years that are coming and store up grain under the authority of Pharaoh for food in the cities, and let them keep it. That food shall be a reserve for the land against the seven years of famine that are to occur in the land of Egypt, so that the land may not perish through the famine.'

"This proposal pleased Pharaoh and all his servants. And Pharaoh said to his servants, 'Can we find a man like this, in whom is the Spirit of God?' Then Pharaoh said to Joseph, 'I have set you over all the land of Egypt.' Then Pharaoh took his signet ring from his hand and put it on Joseph's hand, and clothed him in garments of fine linen and put a gold chain about his neck." (Gen 39:6b–18; 41:14–42)

And from the beginning of Tablet III of the Gilgamesh epic:

"Gilgamesh washed out his long locks and cleaned his weapons; he flung back his hair from his shoulders; he threw off his stained clothes and changed them for new. He put on his royal robes and made them fast. When Gilgamesh had put on the crown, glorious Ishtar lifted her eyes, seeing the beauty of Gilgamesh. She said, 'Come to me Gilgamesh, and be my bridegroom; grant me seed of your body, let me be your bride and you shall be my husband . . .'

"Gilgamesh opened his mouth and answered glorious Ishtar, ' . . . as for making you my wife—that I will not. How would it go with me? . . . if you and I should be lovers, should not I be served in the same fashion as all these others whom you loved once?' When Ishtar heard this she fell into a bitter rage, she went up to high heaven. Her tears poured down in front of her father Anu, and Antum her mother. She said, 'My father, Gilgamesh has heaped insults on me, he has told over all my abominable behavior, my foul and hideous acts . . .

"My father, give me the Bull of Heaven to destroy Gilgamesh. Fill Gilgamesh, I say, with arrogance to his destruction; but if you refuse to give me the Bull of Heaven I will break in the doors of hell and smash the bolts; there will be confusion of people, those above with those from the lower depths. I shall bring up the dead to eat food like the living; and the hosts of dead will outnumber the living.' Anu said to great Ishtar, 'If I do what you desire there will be seven years of drought throughout Uruk when corn will be seedless husks. Have you saved grain enough for the people and grass for the cattle? Ishtar replied, 'I have saved grain for the people, grass for the cattle; for seven years of seedless husks, there is grain and there is grass enough.'"[58]

Some similarities are:

—Gilgamesh is king of Uruk as we saw earlier, and Joseph effectively becomes king of Egypt.

—Gilgamesh is part man, part god. While Joseph is a man, the Spirit of God lives in him.

—Gilgamesh is beautiful, and the goddess Ishtar notices him and asks him to take her for his own. When he refuses, she turns against him and wreaks vengeance on him. Joseph also is well-built and handsome, and Potiphar's wife sees this and asks him to take her for his own. When Joseph refuses she also turns against him and wreaks vengeance on him.

—Gilgamesh washes his hair and changes his clothes, then puts on his royal robes and a crown. Joseph shaves his face and changes his clothes, and Pharaoh puts his signet ring on Joseph's hand, clothes him in garments of fine linen, and puts a gold chain around his neck.

—Anu, the Sumerian god of the heavens, grants the Bull of Heaven to Ishtar and says it will cause seven years of seedless husks, and asks if Ishtar has saved grain for the people for these seven years, which she affirms. In Genesis God uses a dream of seven lean cattle and seven

---

58. Assyrian International News Agency, "Gilgamesh," 12. Some may note parallels here between the Gilgamesh epic and other Scriptures, even from the New Testament.

empty ears of grain to signify that seven years of famine are coming. Joseph advises that grain be stored up for those seven years.

It seems hard to deny that Moses has patterned his account of Joseph on the Gilgamesh epic, but we need not think that the whole biblical account quoted above is purely manufactured, particularly when we read statements such as the following:

> "And Pharaoh called Joseph's name Zaphenath-paneah. And he gave him in marriage Asenath the daughter of Potiphera priest of On. So Joseph went out over the land of Egypt. Joseph was thirty years old when he entered the service of Pharaoh." (Gen 41:45–46)

It seems to me at least that Moses saw parallels between the Gilgamesh epic and his own historical sources about Joseph (which were likely oral, and likely scant on detail),[59] and so he filled in the one using the other.

This is neither dishonest nor unusual in the Ancient Near East, as many of Moses' audience would likely have been familiar with his sources. It's not even unusual now: such works are called historical novels, and they can make a much richer and more meaningful read than plowing through bare and often uncertain facts. Some might not like this designation of Genesis as historical fiction or "filled-in" history. However, it's normal for purely historical works to mention their sources as the books of Kings and Chronicles do, unless of course they are eyewitness accounts. At the very least Moses might have indicated (as did Luke) that there were other accurate accounts around.[60]

It's also possible that God merely dictated Genesis to Moses, and that any similarities with literary works like Gilgamesh are purely coincidental. But then they would be a collected coincidence of miraculous proportions, no better than the "miracle" of evolution. Or perhaps God himself decided to draw deliberate parallels with Gilgamesh. But if God uses the particular personalities and preferences of other biblical writers, and if they in turn use current literary forms and styles (such as Paul's "Grace and peace to

---

59. It's unlikely that any of the patriarchs were literate until Joseph. They had little use for reading and writing, and even less access to them, since they were pastoralists far from court, and the Scriptures were non-existent. One might speculate that Joseph had some family records written down, but when one considers his delicate position both as a Hebrew in an Egyptian court, and among his own brothers (to whom he was trying to bring some stability and reconciliation), this looks less likely given the delicate family matters like illicit intercourse and favoritism that we read about in Genesis.

60. Luke 1:1–3.

you" that adapts both Greek and Hebrew greetings), why can we not allow the same for Moses? It seems that a *human* hand familiar with Ancient Near Eastern literature is in the foreground of Genesis, not the direct mouth of God, and this is the norm in Scripture. Where things have been directly spoken or revealed by God, this is always made clear.[61]

So when we are reading Genesis and perhaps wondering which parts are historical and which parts are fiction, we need to remember that we are dealing with an account that reaches back to the very beginning of the world, and well before the beginning and the spread of writing. The further back we go, the more deeply buried or decomposed the historical content will be, the more Moses must depend on oral and literary accounts of it, and the more gaps he must fill in. As with the legend of King Arthur there is likely true if sparse history in Genesis,[62] and there is literary material that forms part of our past and is (like the historical material) useful for teaching about the richer realm of God and the way for people to enter it and live in it—just as the movie *Life is Beautiful* teaches how to make life the most beautiful when it seems the most horrible. The alternative is to go against Jesus' parable of the wheat and the weeds,[63] and make premature judgements about what is historical and what is not.

So there is nothing unusual or invalid about Moses using the uncertain historical records and literary accounts of the past, which are an unavoidable reality for the era he was dealing with. They are simply vehicles for his real message, which *is* unerring, and which he *is* very careful and precise about, just as Luke and the books of Kings are careful and accurate with their *history*.

So New Testament authors are happy to follow Moses here. When they quote Scripture they are usually happy with whatever Greek translation

---

61. E.g., Deuteronomy 5:4–5; Jeremiah 1:11–14; 1 Corinthians 7:10–12; 2 Peter 1:17–18.

62. For example, Andrew Reid points out that in Genesis 14, "The writing style preserves indications that it is based on very old verse forms . . . the word for 'trained men' (verse 14) is used only here in the Bible, but is found in 18th–19th Century Egyptian inscriptions and 15th Century BC cuneiform inscriptions in Israel . . . The journey followed by the five kings coincides with the Kings Highway, the international caravan route, and speaks of highly developed areas where people live in cities. Archaeological surveys have shown this to be the case between the 21st and 19th centuries BC . . . these same surveys have shown that there was a complete and sudden interruption to such settled life as the result of some catastrophic invasion . . . It is not unreasonable to find in Genesis an authentic echo of this invasion" (*Salvation Begins*, 107–8).

63. Matthew 13:24–30.

they knew or had to hand, rather than determining the pristine original text. When they refer to Scriptural characters and stories they are again typically less concerned with what is historical and more concerned with what we can learn from them.

ACCEPTING PERFECT SCRIPTURES FROM PARTIAL PEOPLE

God is happy to let us discover the natural world and the past for ourselves. His priority is to reveal himself truly and fully so we can know him and worship him. But because of our pride he prefers to do this through people with perspectives that are limited by bent and background, and whose knowledge is limited by their education and their position in history. So when Jesus chose "uneducated, common men" to reveal him to the world,[64] he didn't transform them into scholars of science, Hebrew, or history in the process.[65]

Granted, God also used the educated Paul for his knowledge and grasp of doctrine, and Luke the historian for the sake of our certainty.[66] But God is fully happy with Matthew's zest for seeing fulfillments in Jesus, and with John's love of Jesus' non-literal statements that require reflection and don't promptly slot into our mental grid. Like Luke, the scientifically-minded might prefer a more chronological account of how God created the world. But again like Luke, they must not get hung up about what God has caused to be written already through someone who sees order more in terms of patterns that point to the history-driving ways and purposes of God.

It's always tempting to think that tangible certainties and accuracies will be more compelling to others than our faith in the unseen certainties of God. But our faith is the more compelling, because it makes us live a godly and beautiful life which has no visible cause, just as the beauty in the natural realm is without reason, yet we find it gloriously uplifting.

---

64. Acts 4:13.

65. Even the educated Paul resolved to know nothing among the Corinthians "except Jesus Christ . . . crucified" (1 Cor 2:2).

66. Luke 1:4.

Chapter 4

The Unfolding Image of God

By 2003, we were moving away from a city-based existence and career aspirations. Animals were multiplying in our yard, and our third little boy had recently arrived. So we moved to Tasmania and then to a property in northern New South Wales, to get back to cultivating the earth, husbanding animals, raising children, and generally trying to create our own little bit of Eden. We had some successes, and we have many happy memories: a bumper cauliflower and potato harvest; our "apple room," fragrant from boxes of roadside Tassie apples for cider, and home-grown ones for eating; ample milk and cream from our jersey cow, and so on.

But while it was good for our young family at the time, as a goal for life it was a dead end. It didn't satisfy. And it was work. In the end we got tired of cloth nappies, living in close quarters with farm animals, the fiddly-ness and sometimes downright unpleasantness of not wasting anything, and doing things the "natural" way, which usually meant more work and more yuck.[1] If I had any health problem it was from eating too much healthy food to fill an emptiness inside that wasn't in my stomach.

We felt like less prosperous and less successful versions of Solomon, who after all his efforts to re-create Eden, felt like he had been chasing the wind.[2] Even the wisdom that enabled him to do things well where we had made mistakes, ultimately gave him no satisfaction.[3] He wanted to understand the bigger picture of God's purposes and priorities, so that he

---

1. Like wee-tanning leather and cow poo-and-mud rendering.
2. Ecclesiastes 2:1–11.
3. Ecclesiastes 2:12–17.

could bring some true and lasting progress to the world.[4] In short, one could say that he wanted to grow up, and do real work with real wisdom and real success. But why do we have this longing, so that we wear ourselves out or even kill ourselves trying to do yet more, learn or earn yet more, look or become even better and more famous? Genesis not only answers this question: it also points towards the way this longing can be satisfied, via its teaching about our nature and goal as the image of God.

AN UNFOLDING IMAGE OF GOD FOR AN UNFOLDING NEED OF CREATION

Genesis is very much the story of the central and unfolding role of the image of God, because of the unfolding need of creation. So Moses portrays man as the climax of creation in Genesis 1–2, because he is needed to subdue and govern all the animals, to bring fruitfulness to the barren fields and to God's garden, and to fill the earth with his offspring.[5] But God has granted him the best food (grain and fruit) to enable him to multiply in contrast to the land animals, who are not blessed and are merely given "every green plant."[6]

The book of Genesis as a whole climaxes with Joseph, who shares many parallels with the man of Genesis 1–2. Joseph is entrusted with ruling all of Egypt, which like the portrayal of Eden, was very much the center of civilization and power, and was the garden of the earth during the seven years of plenty (not to mention the pre-eminence of the Nile in the Ancient Near East). Joseph saves Egypt and the surrounding nations and their livestock through the famine, but he particularly blesses the children of Israel by giving them a generous allowance of grain for free, and the best land.[7] This enables Israel to be fruitful and multiply both in the land of Egypt and in comparison to the people of Egypt.[8] Joseph also subdues and governs

---

4. The human difficulty portrayed in Ecclesiastes 3:1–15 is that we don't know which time it is and therefore end up achieving nothing from all our toil. We frequently find that our efforts to save life or save up money are rendered useless by other circumstances, and we now need what we threw away (verses 5–6).
5. Genesis 1:26–30; 2:5, 15.
6. Genesis 1:29–30.
7. Genesis 41:57.
8. Genesis 50:21; Exodus 1:6–7.

his unruly brothers,[9] several of whom are likened to animals in Jacob's blessing.[10] Finally, both Adam and Joseph have a yearning for their own flesh and bone that is eventually satisfied: Adam is joined to the wife who was made from his own body,[11] while Joseph is reunited with his father and brothers.[12]

Noah is a step along the way from Adam to Joseph, as he saves a remnant of human and animal life through the Flood, so that they may be fruitful and multiply after it. This is helped by the fact that through Noah, fruitfulness has been restored to the ground.[13] He also governs all the animals in his care on the ark and provides food for them and for his family, and this governing of the animals extends to people also in that he raises up the righteous and subdues the wicked by his curse and blessing.[14]

Abraham is another step along the way, as in Genesis 14 he defeats the rapacious kings "who lust after tribute"[15] and restores the peoples and property to their rightful place—just as Adam was to subdue and govern both the wild animals and the pushy domestic ones.[16] And through Abraham God subdues the rapacious kings of Egypt and Gerar, and forces them to restore Sarah to her rightful lord[17]—just as David would later rescue the lamb from the mouth of the lion and the bear.

So while Genesis initially connects the image of God with man's ability to reproduce, grow food, and exercise dominion over the animals, it's really pointing the reader onwards to Noah, Abraham, and Joseph. Because in some ways Joseph has become more God-like than Adam was. He has been given dominion over not just animals but people. And while God lies behind Israel's favorable allocation of food in Egypt, it has come through Joseph's initiative. Also, Joseph's yearning for his own flesh and blood is less physical and more gracious than Adam's yearning for a wife, given Adam's later blaming of his wife, and Joseph's earlier treatment at the hands of his

---

9. Genesis 37:5–9; 45:24; 49:3–7.
10. Genesis 49:14–17, 21, 27.
11. Genesis 2:22–24.
12. Genesis 43:30; 45:1–15.
13. Genesis 5:29; 8:21; 9:20.
14. Genesis 9:24–27.
15. Psalm 68:30; Genesis 14:4.
16. Compare the Messiah's role in Ezekiel 34:17–24.
17. Genesis 12:17–20; 20:1–18; 21:22–26.

brothers. Joseph's love for them seems as much a product of his faithfulness to God, as because they are his own flesh and blood.[18]

Finally, there is a contrasting parallel between what makes Adam different from the animals, and what makes Joseph different from his peers. In Genesis 2 God breathes the *breath of life* into Adam, but his likeness to God does not extend beyond the natural realm of having children, ruling the animals, and cultivating and husbanding plants. But Pharaoh recognizes that in Joseph resides the *Spirit of God*, along with a wisdom of divine proportions.[19]

Putting it in terms of Romans 8, God's breath of life enables Adam's physical body, made from the earth, to do and to eat whatever his body feels like, but his earthly mind is still dead in terms of its ability to do what it knows is right. But the Spirit of God has made Joseph's mind alive and able to do what it knows is right, in the face of opposition from the mind of his body, even though it involves a struggle and a sacrifice.[20]

---

18. Genesis 42:18; 50:19–21. The same is true of Judah: his later godliness hints that his initial exhortation that his brothers not kill Joseph because "he is our brother, our own flesh," (Gen 37:27) has come partly from God. At the very least the attitude of Joseph and Judah to their brothers is in contrast to that of their own brothers, and that of Cain and Esau. Similarly, Joseph and Judah's attitude to their father is in contrast to that of Ham (contrast Genesis 9:22 with 44:30–24; 46:29–30; 50:1). So when Elijah comes to "turn the hearts of fathers to their children and the hearts of children to their fathers" (Malachi 4:5–6), he is doing the same thing that the Spirit of God has always done in human hearts. However this needs to be tempered with what we will look at in the next chapter.

19. Genesis 41:38–39. Note that eating from the tree of the knowledge of good and evil, represents man's choice to trust his own wisdom rather than God's. So there is an additional contrast here between Joseph and Adam.

20. So although sin did indeed come into the world through Adam in that he broke God's law (Rom 5:12, 16–19), the deliberate contrast in Genesis between Adam's breath of life and Joseph's Spirit of God indicates that Adam, like his namesake the earth, was initially spiritually barren from the beginning, even though he had not yet sinned and was not yet corrupt. That is, Adam was prone to sin from the beginning like David (Ps 51:5) and us, just as his namesake the earth is prone to produce weeds for man.

This doesn't mean that God's original creation was in any way bad: it was just a beginning, to be transformed into holiness by God's word just as people are. The seventh holy day following the six days of creation makes this divine goal clear from the beginning. This is why Romans 5:12 teaches that death spread to all men not because of Adam's sin, but because of our sin. For Paul there is no mysterious or hidden spiritual (or unspiritual) quality that we inherit from Adam that would have been different if Adam had not sinned. The key thing that Paul teaches as coming into the human world through Adam's sin is death, in the sense of condemnation from God (Rom 5:16, 18; 8:1–3).

True, Romans 5:19 says, "For as by the one man's disobedience the many were made

Therefore the unfolding storyline of Genesis provides growing indications that likeness to God involves more than just the capacities and drives to rule, reproduce, and reap fruit from our work. Cain also grows crops and has children, but his murder of the brother who pleases God shows Cain to be unlike God. Ishmael also seems to despise the brother that God has chosen.[21] Like Cain, Esau wants to kill the brother who is more interested in God's promises than he is, even though Esau is the firstborn heir of them. And there are two rather distinct classes in Jacob's "blessing" on his sons in Genesis 49: there is Judah and Joseph, and there is everyone else. So a fuller significance for the image of God unfolds through Genesis: a likeness to God's nature, generated by the Spirit of God rather than his mere breath of life.

This image continues to unfold through Scripture along the same lines laid down in Genesis, except that because Joseph is still separated from his brothers in relational terms,[22] Jacob is looking to Judah and his offspring[23] as the direction from which order will be brought to the moral chaos, disunity, and spiritual barrenness of the sons of Israel—because it was Judah that the whole family of Israel listened to and followed.[24]

So when God chooses David (a Judahite) to redeem Israel from a similar condition of moral chaos, disunity, and spiritual barrenness,[25] he also is filled with the Spirit,[26] and with a leadership ability of divine proportions. But it's the messianic seed of David who is the true fulfillment of the man in Genesis, so that Isaiah uses the animal and plant imagery of Genesis to picture how the Messiah will subdue and govern the predatory

---

sinners, so by the one man's obedience the many will be made righteous." But this verse is looking back to the previous verse which says, "Therefore, as one trespass led to condemnation for all men . . . ", and this is not saying that Adam's sin *caused* our condemnation, but merely that it *led to it*. This verse is really reiterating what Paul said in Romans 5:12, which is silent about how *sin* spread to all people, but focuses on how Adam's *death* came to us through *our* sin, not his. So in Romans 5:19 the "sinners" and the "righteous" refer not to our inner bent but to our legal standing with regard to the Law that so dominates Paul's discussion in Romans 2–7.

21. Genesis 21:9.
22. Genesis 49:26; 50:15–20.
23. Compare Genesis 49:8–12 with 49:22–26.
24. Including Jacob and Joseph: compare Genesis 37:26–27 with 42:22; 42:37–38 with 43:3, 11; Gen 44:18—45:2.
25. Judges 21:25; 18; 19.
26. 1 Samuel 16:13, 18; 18:7.

nations,[27] bring unity to God's flock (as David did only temporarily),[28] and cause the fruit of righteousness to sprout up in the wilderness (i.e., where there was no righteousness) among all the nations, by the Spirit of God.[29] The Messiah is called the "Branch"[30] because he will produce the fruit of righteousness which is God's true purpose in all the earth,[31] and because the Spirit-empowered leadership ability has passed from Joseph (likened to a branch in Genesis 49) to the messianic seed of Judah. So the image of God continues to unfold through Scripture along the lines laid down in Genesis.

Yet the man who is the image of God is himself a part of God's creation, and so he also is created with a need—for companionship. So just as God "built" a woman out of the man's rib,[32] and later built up Jerusalem the city of David ("the daughter of Zion")[33] around the house of David,[34] so also God is building a temple from his people around Jesus the "cornerstone."[35] So the first man with his wounded side and his wife by his side, are fulfilled in Christ crucified and his bride the church.[36] So if the man is the climax of creation, the building of the woman is the completion of creation, just as the building of the temple is the completion of Israel, and as the church is the completion of Christ, "the fullness of him who fills all in all."[37] So while God's goal for creation has to do with people being transformed into the image of God, it's a corporate goal, not merely for individuals in isolation, but for a united body of people who are together, just as Joseph didn't want his brothers to quarrel but to be united.[38]

---

27. Isaiah 11:4–10.
28. Isaiah 11:12–14; Ezekiel 37:15–22.
29. Isaiah 32:1–2, 15–17; 61:1–3, 11; John 15:4–12.
30. Isaiah 11:1; Jeremiah 23:5.
31. Compare Isaiah 4:2 with 32:16; 45:8; 61:11.
32. Hebrew *banah*—"to build." This is unexpected given the prevalence of "creating," "forming," and "making" terminology in early Genesis—if we are looking for no more than literal history. Hence the NIV and ESV translate *banah* as "made", but the ESV puts the correct translation in a footnote.
33. Biblical Training Institute, "Daughter of Zion."
34. Psalm 147:2; 1 Kings 11:31–32, 36.
35. Ephesians 2:19–22; 1 Peter 2:4–7.
36. Law, *Gospel in Genesis*, 26; Ephesians 5:31–32.
37. Ephesians 1:23.
38. Genesis 45:24; 42:22–24.

A THREEFOLD IMAGE OF A THREEFOLD GOD

But what is the shape of this image of God that we see the Spirit creating in these men? In short, it is a threefold role of prophet-priest-king, and this should come as no surprise given that it reflects the triune God: the Spirit of prophecy, the priesthood of Jesus, and the headship and authority of the Father.[39]

So Abraham, the father of all believers, is called a prophet.[40] Genesis also portrays his kingly wealth,[41] and his kingly power in defeating a coalition of five kings in Genesis 1. Abimelech the king of Gerar makes a treaty with him as with an equal,[42] and the Hittites regard him as "a mighty prince."[43] Regarding Abraham's priesthood, he serves dinner to the angel of the Lord just as the later Israelite priests served God at close quarters and put out bread for him. He also intercedes for Lot,[44] mediates between God and Abimelech,[45] builds altars,[46] and makes a burnt offering to God.[47]

Noah receives a similar priestly portrayal. As with Abraham, Noah's final deed which brought on God's blessing and covenant, was to build an altar and make burnt offerings to God.[48] He also blesses and curses on God's behalf,[49] and he occupies a mediating position between God and his creation. These again are priestly activities and roles.

Regarding Noah's kingly role, he stands at the head of the first family after the Flood, and he gives dominion to the line of his eldest son. Moses says nothing about Noah's prophetic role, but Joseph is a prophet as he reveals the future via dreams. Joseph is also "like Pharaoh" in his kingly authority, but there is nothing especially priestly in his portrayal. But Moses and David strongly fill out all three roles: the prophetic role of speaking

---

39. 1 Corinthians 11:3; 15:28.
40. Genesis 20:7.
41. Genesis 12:16; 13:2, 6.
42. Genesis 21:22–32.
43. Genesis 23:6.
44. Genesis 18.
45. Genesis 20:7, 17.
46. Genesis 12:8; 13:18; 22:9.
47. Genesis 22:9–13.
48. Genesis 8:20.
49. Genesis 9:25–27.

for God,[50] the priestly role of interceding, mediating, blessing, and offering sacrifices,[51] and the kingly role of ruling and leading Israel.[52] It's God's purpose that Israel also fill out these roles:

> "Now therefore, if you will indeed obey my voice and keep my covenant, you shall be my treasured possession among all peoples, for all the earth is mine; and you shall be to me a dominion of priests and a holy nation." (Exod 19:5–6)

> "But Moses said to [Joshua] . . . 'Would that all the Lord's people were prophets, that the Lord would put his Spirit on them.'" (Num 11:29)

> "And it shall come to pass afterward that I will pour out my Spirit on all flesh; your sons and your daughters shall prophesy, your old men shall dream dreams, and your young men shall see visions. Even on the male and female servants in those days I will pour out my Spirit." (Joel 2:28–29)

The book of Revelation, which gives a glimpse of God's goal for man fulfilled, also emphasizes these three roles of prophet, priest, and king, particularly in chapter 11 where the church is represented as two witnesses:[53]

> "And I will grant authority to my two witnesses, and they will prophesy for 1,260 days, clothed in sackcloth. These are the two olive trees and the two lampstands that stand before the Lord of all the earth. And if anyone would harm them, fire pours from their mouth and consumes their foes . . . They have the power to shut the sky, that no rain may fall during the days of their prophesying, and they have power over the waters to turn them into blood and to strike the earth with every kind of plague, as often as they desire." (Rev 11:3–6)

---

50. Deuteronomy 18:15–20.

51. Exodus 20:18–21; 32:30–32; Numbers 12:7–13; Deuteronomy 33:1; 2 Samuel 16:17–20; chapter 24.

52. Compare Exodus 18:13; 32:20.

53. Because in matters of judgement and therefore prophetic testimony and intercession (whether to judge or save), everything must be confirmed by the testimony of two or three witnesses (Deut 19:15; Matt 18:16, 18–20; John 5:30–37; 2 Cor 13:1–5). The number two is chosen here because it matches the two olive trees in Zechariah that the passage alludes to.

While this passage is explicit about the church's prophetic role, its priestly and kingly roles are expressed via the two olive trees and lampstands. These allude to Zechariah 4 in which Zerubbabel, the Davidic governor of Judah,[54] is likened to a lampstand filled with oil, with the potential that he similarly be filled with the Spirit like his ancestor David. Zerubbabel is also likened with Joshua the high priest to a pair of olive trees that grow next to this lampstand, and so the above passage in Revelation is alluding to both the priestly and kingly role for God's people. While prophecy is the dominant role given to God's people in Revelation,[55] this twin role of priest-king is never far below the surface, and is occasionally made more explicit:

> "To him who loves us and has freed us from our sins by his blood and made us a kingdom, priests to his God and father . . . " (Rev 1:5–6)

> "And you have made them a kingdom and priests to our God, and they shall reign on the earth." (Rev 5:10)

> "They will be priests of God and of Christ, and they will reign with him for a thousand years." (Rev 20:6)

In summary, Moses seems to have presented Noah, Abraham, and Joseph for Israel and for us to imitate and meditate on, because God's goal for Israel and us is to bear his triune image. Moses makes this goal initially attractive for us in Genesis by also portraying the material prosperity, fruitfulness, and authority of these men. But increasingly as we move through biblical history, this fruitfulness, prosperity, and authority move into either the spiritual realm, or into the future age. Consider the call of Jeremiah:

> "The words of Jeremiah, the son of Hilkiah, one of the priests . . . 'Before I formed you in the womb I knew you, and before you were born I consecrated you; I appointed you a prophet to the nations' . . . 'I have set you this day over nations and over kingdoms, to pluck up and to break down, to destroy and to overthrow, to build and to plant.'" (Jer 1:5, 10)

While Jeremiah's prophetic and priestly roles are self-evident, his kingly role is seen in the authority and power he has been given by God. Yet he occupies no earthly position of authority or power, and is constantly

---

54. Haggai 1:1.
55. E.g., Revelation 10.

vulnerable to those in such positions. He is forbidden to marry and have children,[56] he is widely rejected, he is dependent on others for food,[57] and he ultimately fails to turn Israel back to God. The same is true of Jesus: at the end of his life he had no children, no wealth, no position, no family honor, and no success with Israel. Suffering and dishonor are the hallmarks of all who follow him,[58] like Paul the apostle.[59]

So Genesis 1–3 uses agricultural, environmental, and family aspirations to draw Israel into God's higher purpose of creating children in his triune image, as with Noah, Abraham, Jacob, and Joseph. But what does it mean for us to be images of God now? We look at what it means to be a prophet and a priest in chapter 7. As a king it means bringing justice to those under our power or care, especially preventing the weak from being exploited.[60]

HOLY IMAGE OF A HOLY GOD

We saw earlier that the six days of creation and the seventh unending day of holiness are a parable of God's work in this world from its beginning to its end, when holiness will have filled the earth and there will be nothing left that is unclean or ungodly.[61] But how will God get his creation to this goal? The means that Genesis 1 indicates is the man whom God creates as his image, who will subdue all that is violent and rapacious, and fill the earth with his offspring.[62] Isaiah indicates that this figure is marked above all by righteousness,[63] so it is no surprise that righteousness is another key aspect to the unfolding image of God in Genesis. Joseph remains blameless in the face of strong temptations to adultery, revenge on his brothers, and disobedience to his father. He probably knew what to expect when his father sent

---

56. Jeremiah 16:1–2.
57. Jeremiah 37:21.
58. E.g., 1 Peter 4.
59. In 1 Corinthians 4:8–13, Paul teaches both the need for suffering and dishonor in the present age, and the hope of kingly authority and wealth in the coming age—"*Already* you have all you want! *Already* you have become rich! Without us you have become kings! And would that you did reign, so that we might share the rule with you!"
60. As the Messiah does in Isaiah 11 and 42. See also Proverbs 31:1–9.
61. Compare Revelation 21:27; 22:15.
62. Compare Isaiah 11:1–13; 65:17, 23–25.
63. Isaiah 11:4–5.

him to visit his brothers at Shechem, yet he obediently went.[64] Even when he didn't find his brothers there and had an excuse to come home, he stuck to his errand to its bitter end.[65]

Once again, Noah and Abraham are steps along the way from Adam to Joseph. Noah was righteous and blameless,[66] but at the end he gets drunk and uncovers himself. Abraham's story ends on a higher note than Noah's but he stumbles more along the way. When the nation of Israel is being born, God fully reveals his goal for them of holiness:

> "Now therefore, if you will indeed obey my voice and keep my covenant,[67] you shall be my treasured possession among all peoples, for all the earth is mine; and you shall be to me a dominion of priests and a holy nation." (Exod 19:5-6)

The New Testament confirms that God has not moved on from this goal of holiness, either for individuals[68] or for the world.[69] Filling the earth with holy offspring means teaching and training our children or disciples in the way of Jesus' commands,[70] rather than raising children who are merely good leaders, or socially well-adjusted, emotionally secure, or prosperous.

BEING A SON BUT NOT SPOUTING ABOUT IT

At one of the colleges where I studied there was a lecturer who was highly regarded by the students. His son was quiet and content, and didn't volunteer anything about his father or about home life. We had a heifer calf who was similar. We rarely saw her drinking, and we never saw her looking or sounding needy, which was quite a contrast with the orphaned calf we were trying to share her mum with. He got through alright, but he had it a bit tough. But both that son and that heifer calf left an impression on me. They obviously enjoyed an intimate relationship with those who had given them

---

64. Genesis 37:12–14.
65. Genesis 37:15–17.
66. Genesis 6:9.
67. A dual reference to the Ten Commandments in particular, which Israel would hear directly from God and which formed the heart of the covenant.
68. E.g., Matthew 5:17–48; Ephesians 1:4; 4:24; Hebrews 12:14;1 Peter 1:14–16.
69. Matthew 6:9–10.
70. Malachi 2:15; Matthew 28:19–20; Ephesians 6:4. See also the quote from Exodus above.

The Unfolding Image of God

life and continued to nourish it, but it was a private affair. We see a similar reality associated closely with the image of God in Genesis via the idea of creating:

> "So God *created* man in his own image; in the image of God he *created* him, male and female he *created* them." (Gen 1:27)

The Hebrew word involved here is *bara'*—but what does it mean? Some have thought that it means "to create out of nothing," given its use in Genesis 1:1 ("God *created* the heavens and the earth"). But this seems unlikely given that God also *created* man, yet formed him from the ground in Genesis 2. In Isaiah 40–45 (the other main place where *bara'* occurs in Scripture), the really prominent sense is of God's *sole responsibility* for and *intimate involvement* with what he has made or done:

—"Lift up your eyes on high and see: who *created* these [stars]? He who brings out their host by number, *calling them all by name* . . . *not one is missing*" (40:26) [i.e., *God* made them, and he knows them *intimately*]

—"that they may see and know, may consider and understand together, that *the hand of the Lord* has done this, the Holy One of Israel has *created* it." (41:20)

—"But now thus says the Lord, he who *created* you, O Jacob, he who formed you, O Israel: 'Fear not, for *I* have redeemed you; *I* have called you by name, you are mine.'" (43:1)

—" . . . everyone who is *called by my name*, whom I *created* for my glory, whom *I* formed and made." (43:7)

—"*I* am the Lord, *your* Holy One, the *Creator* of Israel, *your* king." (43:15)

—"*I* form light and *create* darkness, *I* make well-being and *create* calamity, *I am the* Lord, who does all these things." (45:7)

—"let the earth open, that salvation and righteousness may bear fruit; let the earth cause them both to sprout; *I the* Lord have *created* it." (45:8)

—"*I* made the earth and *created* man on it; it was *my* hands that stretched out the heavens, and *I* commanded all their host." (45:12)

—"For thus says the Lord, who *created* the heavens (*he* is God!), who formed the earth and made it (*he* established it)." (45:18)

These meanings of intimate involvement and sole responsibility fit nicely in Genesis 1:1, because verse 2 goes on to say that the Spirit of God was fluttering over the waters—just as God's care of Israel is likened to an eagle fluttering over its young in the Song of Moses.[71] This "fluttering" word (Hebrew *raḥaph*) occurs only in these two places in Scripture, which strengthens the connection between *baraʾ* and God's intimate involvement with what he creates. In the Song of Moses also, God's sole responsibility for creating Israel and his intimate involvement with them are both prominent themes.

These themes are also associated with the next occurrence of *baraʾ* in Genesis 1:21 where God creates the sea creatures and birds, because God goes on to bless them. It's also worth noting that the list of creatures God creates here is headed by the "great sea creatures" (Hebrew *tannînîm*, also translated as monsters or dragons), and that elsewhere in Scripture God has a special interest in them.[72]

So when Moses uses *baraʾ* three times in Genesis 1:27 to refer to God's creation of man as his image, Moses is triply underlining God's sole responsibility for and intimate involvement with man as the image of God. The verse is immediately followed by God blessing them and speaking to them about their food and the food of the animals they will govern. And in the next chapter we see God shaping a body for man out of the soil and breathing life into him. All this strongly emphasizes God's personal, intimate involvement in making man as his image, and his sole responsibility for it.

This almost over-emphasized intimate involvement and sole responsibility of God in making someone in his image, indicates the relationship that a father has with his son. Just to be sure that we get this point, Moses adds,

> "When God created man, he made him in the likeness of God . . . When Adam had lived one hundred and thirty years, he fathered a son in his own likeness, after his image, and named him Seth" (Gen 5:1, 3).

So God's goal for Adam as his image and likeness, was to be his own son, just as it was his goal for Solomon:

> "[God] said to me, 'It is Solomon your son who shall build my house and my courts, for I have chosen him to be my son, and I will be his father. I will establish his kingdom forever if he

---

71. Deuteronomy 32:10–12.
72. E.g., Psalm 104:25–26; Job 41.

continues strong in keeping my commandments and my rules, as he is today.'" (1 Chr 28:6–7)

So the primary identity of Jesus, the image and likeness of God,[73] is as the son of God, and both John and Paul are clear that God's ultimate goal for us is to be his children.[74]

This sole responsibility of God for creating us means that the first cause of every child of God is not the word of God but the choice of God. There is no material precedent, so throughout Genesis we see some people turn towards God from nondescript parents, and others turning away from God despite godly parents.

Religion also provides no precedent. It was Cain who initiated sacrificing to God, and it was Moses' and Jeremiah's fellow priests and Levites who most opposed them[75] (not to mention Jesus' clash with the temple hierarchy and the Pharisees).

This intimate involvement by which God creates his children indicates that he requires our own intimacy with him, in contrast with Adam who tried to hide from God, and Cain who tried to hide the truth from him. It is also worth noting that when Jesus underlines this openness and closeness (i.e., intimacy) with God, the theme of God's sole responsibility for his children also surfaces:

> "Everyone who does wicked things hates the light and does not come to the light, lest his works should be exposed. But whoever does what is true comes to the light, so that it may be clearly seen that his works have been carried out in God." (John 3:20–21)

We see this intimacy in Genesis in that Enoch, Noah, and Abraham all "walked with God."[76] Yet God's intimacy reaches out to sinners too: he calls to Adam to walk with him, and he knows what Cain is thinking, and speaks to bring him back into the way.[77]

But this intimacy with God is not something that God's children want to make public, just as husbands and wives who love each other keep their intimacy private. So in Numbers 12 where Miriam and Aaron challenge Moses, he is too meek to say anything on his own behalf, but God reveals

---

73. John 14:9; 2 Corinthians 3:18; Hebrews 1:3.
74. Romans 8:29; 1 John 3:1–2.
75. E.g., Numbers 12 & 16.
76. Genesis 5:24; 6:9; 18:16.
77. Genesis 3:8–9; 4:6–7.

his uniquely intimate relationship with Moses—and therefore Moses' unique qualification for revealing God—to put Miriam and Aaron back in their place. This is partly why Jesus says, "No one knows the Son except the Father, and no one knows the Father except the Son, and anyone to whom the Son chooses to reveal him" (Matt 11:27).

No one except the Father knows the fullness of Jesus' relationship with him—and Jesus is happy to keep it that way for the moment.[78] But it does uniquely qualify Jesus to reveal his Father. The situation is similar in 2 Corinthians 11–12. Paul's super-spiritual opponents seem to boast of their visions and revelations, but Paul has said nothing about his vision for fourteen years, and he distances himself from it by saying instead that he knew a man who had this vision. One reason for this is Paul's awareness that what God has publicly revealed for all to see and hear—the gospel of Christ—is enough for our salvation.

The question then is whether any special vision or revelation we have is for everyone, or only for ourselves. Vomit is a fitting description for revelations or visions that are barely digested for personal nourishment before they are brought up and out for everyone. Or one little vision and then out comes the book, the movie, and the true and full revelation of God in Christ is set aside and forgotten.

But after Ezekiel had seen the vision and eaten the revelation, he sat overwhelmed for seven days, and was forbidden to speak other than to pass on God's "words of lamentation and mourning and woe" and warning.[79] So a safe criterion for whether to share our visions and revelations with others is whether it will raise or lower us in their eyes. We might honor Isaiah as one of the greats, but his having to walk around Jerusalem butt-naked for three years is probably not a favorite subject of meditation for most of us.[80] Therefore Paul chose to boast of his weaknesses, and deemed that his vision was an intimate thing for himself alone.

Another particular area of intimacy with God is prayer, so that Jesus said, "When you pray, go into the room and shut the door."[81] But photographs of people praying are like pornography: they are invasive to the person talking intimately with God, and they feed a desire or pressure to look good and perform for other eyes. This is spiritual adultery. Yes, there is

---

78. 1 John 3:2.
79. Ezekiel 2–3; quoted verse is 2:10.
80. Isaiah 20:1–3.
81. Matthew 6:6.

a place for public prayer, but this is for building up others,[82] not to express our own supposedly intimate relationship.

In conclusion, the essence of the image of God is sonship, which involves God's sole responsibility for creating us, and his intimate involvement in growing us up. But intimacy is mutual, and so we must not hide from God when we are guilty. But we should hide our intimacy with him from others unless it is about our weaknesses and failures, so that it won't boost our own name but will hopefully build others up.

GROWING UP OR GOING BACK

Although we no longer live in Eden, the book of Ecclesiastes emphasizes that we are to enjoy whatever pleasure we get from its particular blessings of work, wealth, food, and family.[83] But when we seek to become great experts and make great achievements in these small matters, and turn aside from our main business of knowing and becoming like the God who created us, it turns us into fools.[84] Accordingly, we cringe when we hear people speaking of and living for small things with great earnestness, especially when they are overlooking more pressing needs like earning a living, loving their wife, giving time to their kids and grand-kids, or helping out someone who needs it.

But as in Eden and as in the parable of the rich fool, God takes away the life he gave us when we turn away from divine wisdom to pursue its worldly alternative.[85] Another way that God takes away our life is by turning these higher desires and this divine potential into thinking and behavior that are worse than the worst that we see in animals,[86] just as Israel became more corrupt and foolish than the surrounding nations who had not known God.

God's wisdom is learned via keeping his commands. To put it another way, our nature is transformed by the same word of God that transforms and orders creation in Genesis 1. Accordingly, turning away from God and his goal for us always involves breaking his commands, and so the

---

82. John 11:42.

83. Compare Genesis 1:28; 2:12, 15, 23; Ecclesiastes 2:24; 3:13, 22; 5:18–20; 8:15; 9:7–10; 11:9.

84. Romans 1:21–23; Luke 12:18–20.

85. Genesis 3; Luke 12:15–21. Cf. also Judas.

86. Romans 1:21–31.

summary exhortation of Ecclesiastes is to keep them, "for this is the whole duty of man."[87]

So given the whole purpose that we are "wired" for, the attempt to create an Eden in this life without God is inevitably futile and unsatisfying. Looking back on our time in Tasmania and on the family farm, it had its pleasures and we have special memories, but there is an overall sense of so much fruitless effort and that there is no going back.

---

87. Ecclesiastes 12:13; see also 1 Corinthians 7:19..

Chapter 5

Seed and Soil that Speak of Salvation

ONE DAY SEEMINGLY OUT of the blue, Jesus told a story about seed that was sown in four different sorts of soil, and what became of them. It was more of a stylized story than a scientific one, in that three of the four kinds of soil produced nothing and the fourth kind produced everything, whereas normally there's more gradation. Jesus' disciples were discerning enough to guess that more was being taught here than mere agriculture, and Jesus recognized this. Even so, his response might seem severe at first glance:

> "To you has been given the secret of the kingdom of God, but for those outside everything is in parables, so that 'they may indeed see but not perceive, and may indeed hear but not understand, lest they should turn and be forgiven.' Do you not understand this parable? How then will you understand all the parables?" (Mark 4:11–13)

Two things are evident here, yet perhaps not understood. One is that Jesus expected his disciples to recognize what he was talking about, and the other is that there is something foundational about the parable of the sower. A third thing that becomes evident as we read on in Matthew and Mark is that the sower is the first of four parables that share the same theme of seed growing into plants. The other parables are of the wheat and the tares (also known as the weeds or the harvest), the growing seed, and the mustard seed.[1] These three things begin to make sense when we think about the creation of plant life in Genesis:

---

1. Matthew 13:24–32; Mark 4:26–32.

"And God said, 'Let the earth sprout vegetation; small plants yielding seed, and fruit trees bearing fruit in which is their seed, each according to its kind, on the earth.' And it was so. The earth brought forth vegetation; small plants yielding seed according to their own kinds, and trees bearing fruit in which is their seed, each according to its kind . . . And God said, 'Behold, I have given you every plant yielding seed that is on the face of the earth, and every tree with seed in its fruit. You shall have them for food.'" (Gen 1:11–12, 29)

Again it's a stylized rather than scientific account. Important plant groups even from Ancient Near Eastern botany don't seem to fit into either of these categories, like the "small plants"[2] and vines that also grow fruit containing seed (e.g., grapes and the cucumber family), and the conifers which are trees but grow cones rather than fruit. One might argue that Moses regarded cones as technically a fruit, but this is unlikely given his emphasis here on the food value of plants rather than their other products like fuel, fabrics, timber, and medicine. Like the parables mentioned earlier there is also an emphasis on seed, which becomes more important as we read on in Genesis:

"Closely linked to the genealogical structure of Genesis is the frequent use of the Hebrew word *zeraʿ*[3] which is perhaps best translated as 'seed'. Unfortunately, the NIV translates *zeraʿ* using a variety of terms—the most common being 'descendants', 'offspring', 'seed', 'children', 'family', 'grain', 'semen' . . . For this reason the importance of the concept of 'seed' in Genesis is easily missed. *Zeraʿ* is a keyword . . . occurring 59 times in Genesis compared to 170 times in the rest of the Old Testament."[4]

Outside of Genesis 1, all but five of these occurrences of *zeraʿ* in Genesis refer to human offspring, and the bulk of these occur in God's promises to bless Abraham, Isaac, and Jacob with offspring, and with land and dominion for their offspring.[5] This is a strong indication that the creation of plants in Genesis 1 is foundational for understanding the rest of the "seed"

---

2. I.e., non-perennials (Holladay, *Hebrew and Aramaic Lexicon*, 284, middle of right hand column). See also ESV footnote for Genesis 1:11.

3. The apostrophe is not pronounced, but represents the Hebrew letter Aleph.

4. Alexander, *From Paradise to the Promised Land*, 103.

5. Look for "offspring," descendants," or "children" in God's speeches in Genesis 13, 15, 17, 22, 26, 28, 48.

theology of Genesis, just as the parable of the sower is foundational for understanding the rest of Jesus' parables.

If this is true, Jesus' reply to the disciples becomes more understandable: if they had missed the "seed" theology of Genesis 1, would they think any more deeply about his parables? So in this chapter we look at the various things Genesis 1 teaches using this idea of seed, and how it unfolds through Genesis and the rest of Scripture.

THE FEW THAT FILL THE EARTH, EVENTUALLY

The general picture in Genesis 1–2 is of God creating only a few of each kind of life which, with his blessing, would fill the earth. This is clear enough with sea creatures, birds, and people, who are blessed and told to "Be fruitful and multiply and fill" the seas and the earth.[6] But in Genesis 2 the land animals are portrayed as being formed in the same way as the birds: "So out of the ground the LORD God formed every beast of the field and every bird of the heavens and brought them to the man to see what he would call them" (Gen 2:19).

This makes it more likely that the land animals were also created few in number, and the sense here is indeed that God created a small number of animals, just enough for Adam to meet and name them, and enough for them to breed and multiply. This would parallel the Flood narrative where the earth was repopulated by just two of each animal.[7] Given this context, Moses' emphasis that the small plants and fruit trees were created bearing seed, hints that the different plant kinds were also initially created few in number, with God's intention that their seed would multiply them.[8]

A particular feature of plants as opposed to animals is the large amount of potential offspring they produce. Even the largest litters of animals don't come near the seasonal output of seed for most plants. But a plant's actual offspring of seedlings is often delayed. While animals produce embryos that generally start growing right away,[9] plant embryos usually end up lying dormant much longer. But if conditions are right, one can end up with

---

6. Genesis 1:22, 28.

7. According to the narrative, although Noah preserved seven of every "clean" animal, he sacrificed some of each of these afterwards, so there might not have been many more than two left.

8. Cf. Atkinson, *Genesis 1–11*, top of page 29.

9. Although eggs have to be incubated.

a lot of seedlings from just one plant. Even after a plant has died, seedlings can keep coming up in large numbers for a long time after, and reproducing in turn.

This situation is similar to God's promise to Abraham (inherited by Isaac and Jacob) which so dominates Genesis:[10] they would ultimately have offspring as numerous as the sand on the seashore and as the stars in the heavens, but it wouldn't be for a while. Moses seems to have portrayed the creation of plants as a sign of God's promise to Abraham and his heirs that despite appearances, God would multiply them abundantly.

But Abraham's true heirs are not merely biological: they are those who have followed in the footsteps of his faith and righteousness,[11] and the real multitudes of these have only come in much later. Similarly, Jesus' offspring are spiritual rather than biological,[12] and they didn't really start to multiply until after his death: "When you make his life an offering for sin, he will see his offspring; he will prolong his days" (Isa 53:10).

So God's blessing that multiplies the offspring of the righteous, means that it is not a matter of cause and effect, of simply learning "discipling" skills and expecting prompt results. We need to resist the temptation to use any pressure, manipulation, or dishonesty, and we must not be deceived into thinking we *have* made disciples because they have "come forward," made a "decision," or have been baptized. We should expect that our true offspring will not show itself till much later, partly because it's our deeds that will be remembered longest and have the greatest influence, and this brings us to another use of the seed and fruit science in Genesis.

THE SEEDS IN OUR DEEDS

Why does Moses so emphasize that the seed of a fruit tree is in its fruit?

> "... fruit trees bearing fruit in which is their seed ... trees bearing fruit in which is their seed ... every tree with seed in its fruit." (Gen 1:11, 12, 29)

A good place to start looking for answers is where fruit next features in Genesis—where the man and woman eat from the forbidden tree. Here, a close connection is drawn between eating fruit and the long term and

---

10. Genesis 12:2; 15:5; 17:5–6; 22:17; 26:4; 28:14; 35:11; 47:27.
11. Matthew 3:9; Romans 4:11–12; 9:6–29; Galatians 3:7, 29.
12. Hebrews 2:10–16.

Seed and Soil that Speak of Salvation

spreading outcome of one's conduct and decisions. When Adam eats from the forbidden tree, there quickly follow shame, blame, and the curse of God. In chapter 4 we see worse things spreading down through the generations: anger, murder, lying, violence, boasting, and an intensification of God's curse. In Genesis 5 we see death spreading to all people, and in chapter 6 we see that corruption and violence have also spread to all people,[13] all from eating a piece of fruit. But Moses wants us to be aware that it had seed in it. In other words, seemingly small matters of disobedience (or obedience) contain seeds that grow and spread into larger things, just as a single plant or animal enters a new environment and grows and spreads till it becomes a major problem.

But eating from the forbidden tree was not just an act of disobedience. It's also portrayed as a fruit of unbelief, because eating from the tree of the knowledge of good and evil means deciding that we need to taste and know for ourselves the good or evil of things that God already knows about,[14] and has already told us are bad. Put simply, we don't believe God.

It's not surprising then that one of the key points in Genesis where this Fall of Man begins to be reversed, is where Abraham believes God and God counts it as righteousness.[15] But the central point of this reversal is where Abraham's faith ripens into his obedience to God's command to sacrifice Isaac:[16]

> "And Isaac said to his father Abraham . . . 'Behold, the fire and the wood, but where is the lamb for a burnt offering?' Abraham said, 'God will provide for himself the lamb for a burnt offering, my son.' . . . 'By myself I have sworn, declares the LORD, because you have done this and have not withheld your son, your only son, I will surely bless you, and I will surely multiply your seed as the stars of heaven and as the sand that is on the seashore. And your seed will possess the gate of his/their enemies, and in your seed will all the nations of the earth be blessed, because you have obeyed my voice." (Gen 22:7–8, 15–18)

So God's curse that spreads to all men through one act of disobedience is replaced by a blessing that will spread to all nations through one act of

---

13. Paul sums it up well: "sin came into the world through one man, and death through sin, and so death spread to all men, because all sinned" (Rom 5:12)
14. "You will be like God, knowing good and evil" (Gen 3:5).
15. Genesis 15:6.
16. James 2:22–23.

obedience, and through the seed of the man that did it. So in Genesis 1, Moses may be preparing us to understand that it's our fully matured and ripened fruit of trusting obedience—of righteousness—that will produce seeds that grow up into children of God. At least this seems to be what Jesus teaches in the parable of the sower:[17]

> "And some fell into good soil and grew and yielded a hundredfold ... And as for what fell among the thorns, they are those who hear, but as they go on their way they are choked by the cares and riches and pleasures of life, and their fruit does not mature. As for that in the good soil, they are those who, hearing the word, hold it fast in an honest and good heart, and bear fruit with endurance." (Luke 8:8, 14–15)

The fruit here is the consequence of a righteousness that ripens through endurance, and the reference to "a hundredfold" indicates that this fruit is also identified with abundant spiritual offspring. Just as unripe fruit has less or no viable seed, so also if our faith is not fully ripened into obedience through suffering it produces little if any offspring.

DIFFERENT SEED THAT DOESN'T MIX

The creation of plants in Genesis 1 indicates another reason why there is a clear boundary between those whom God blesses and those he does not bless. It does so via the repeated refrain "each according to its kind," which occurs three times at the creation of plants, and another four times at the

---

17. Both secular and Scriptural writers like to compare righteous people with flourishing and fruitful trees. The Egyptian *Instruction of Amenemopet* seems to be the earliest known example, dating from around 1300 BC to 1000 BC (Wikipedia, *Instruction of Amenemope*; Lundbom, *Jeremiah 1–20*, 781). Whether or not this is the sole inspiration for the Scriptural writers, they seem to have found it adaptable to their own priorities, notably righteousness and faith (Pss 1; 52:8; 92:12–14; Jeremiah 17:5–8). Other Scriptures that connect fruit with righteousness are Isaiah 5:1–7; 11:1, 4–5; John 15:5, 9–10; Matthew 3:8–9; 7:15–23.

In this last passage the ESV refers to these trees as healthy or diseased, and their fruit as bad in the sense of rotten—instead of referring to the trees as good or unwholesome, and their fruit as evil (the more literal translation). But Jesus is not talking about trees that are healthy or diseased: he is talking about trees that cannot bear fruit because they never were fruit trees. They are thorn bushes and thistles. The people Jesus is referring to here are not bad in the sense of being diseased, but in the sense of being evil. The ESV translation obscures the moral dimension that Jesus is underlining.

Seed and Soil that Speak of Salvation

creation of the animals.[18] The point may be that as with plants and animals, there is a sharp dividing line between different kinds of people which is preserved in their offspring. This prepares us for understanding how God's curse on the serpent will work out: "I will put enmity between you and the woman, and between your seed and her seed; he will bash your head, and you will bash his heel" (Gen 3:15, own translation).

From this point onward in Genesis there is nothing about strife between serpents and people, but there is plenty of opposition between brothers. Cain murders righteous Abel, Shem and Ham have opposite attitudes to their father and to purity, Esau and Jacob have opposite views about the divine promises they stand to inherit, and at one stage Esau wants to kill Jacob. The final narrative in Genesis is dominated by the contrast and conflict between righteous Joseph and his brothers, who again want to kill him at one stage.

These people all reproduce according to their kind, and as with inbreeding, their particular traits are often intensified down their line of descent. Cain's murderous and self-justifying likeness is intensified in Lamech, Ham's corruption intensifies in his descendants at Sodom and Gomorrah, and Esau's uneasy relationship with Jacob further deteriorates among his descendants.[19] Also, the line of descent from Adam the image of God through Seth the image of Adam,[20] continues to produce people who are increasingly outstanding for their righteousness, notably Noah and Joseph.

The consistent picture here is that offspring go one way or the other, and that when all boils down there are only two kinds.[21] One group falls away from God's purposes, while others are included and brought up into them. So Abraham, Isaac, Jacob, and Judah all initially commit the usual sins of their generation, yet God speaks with them and/or disciplines their errors, and so brings them into his way. So the different kinds of people and lines of descent in Genesis have nothing to do with biology.

Genesis 1 goes further and indicates that it's *good* if these different kinds don't mix, because one kind is good and the other is bad, and the

---

18. Genesis 1:11–12, 24–25.
19. E.g., Psalm 137:7. There was a brief alliance in 2 Kings 3.
20. Genesis 4:25—5:3.
21. Accordingly, "fish of every kind" are caught in the parable of the Net, but men sort them into just "good" and "bad," and this refers to the final judgement people (Matt 13:47–49).

good is spoiled if they mix together. Genesis 1 indicates this by its use of the refrain "God saw that it was good." The first time this refrain occurs is when God sees that the light is good.[22] He immediately responds by separating the light from the darkness. In the second half of the creation week when God makes the two great lights, his final purpose for them is "to separate the light from the darkness. And God saw that it was good" (Gen 1:18). So once again the refrain of God seeing that his work is good, is especially associated with his keeping the good and bad separate. So it comes as no surprise that other Scriptural writers use this separation of good light and bad darkness to teach about God's righteous people being separated from partnership and fellowship with the wicked.[23]

One could argue that Moses was being literal here while Isaiah, Jesus, and Paul (among others) all exercise their creative freedom to apply him metaphorically, but this seems unlikely for two reasons. One is that they all apply the light/dark metaphor in the same way, and the other is that their stated intention elsewhere is always to be faithful to Moses' true intent.[24] This indicates that they have all judged Moses to be speaking metaphorically here about people rather than light as such.

The second time that God sees his work as good is when he gathers the waters away so that dry land appears. While this "gathering" rather than "separating" terminology is probably meant to indicate the drowning of Pharaoh's army in the Red Sea, a separation of land and sea is also in view. This is like the Exodus, where not only was Pharaoh's army drowned, but through this Israel was brought out of Egypt, just as the earth was brought up out of the water. These categories of land and seas, like light and darkness, are also used elsewhere in Scripture to refer to God's righteous people on the one hand, and the nations that oppose them on the other.[25]

This background indicates that when God looks on his work of creating plants and animals and sees that it is good, he has in mind especially that different kinds have been kept separate. In that case, this teaching of the plant passage fits in nicely with the broader teaching of Genesis, that maintaining boundaries between different kinds of people is good and

---

22. Genesis 1:4.

23. Compare Isaiah 9:1–2; 60:1–3, 9; 61:3, 10–11; 62:1–3; Matthew 5:14–16; Romans 13:12–13; Ephesians 5:6–14; Philippians 2:14; Colossians 1:12–13.

24. E.g., Isaiah 8:19–20; Matthew 19:4–8; John 5:39–46; 1 Corinthians 9:8–10.

25. Notably Daniel 7:2–6, 17; Revelation 12:15—113:2; see also Psalm 69:1–4, 14–15.

Seed and Soil that Speak of Salvation

necessary, because it helps to prevent God's people being led astray,[26] and it helps to ensure offspring who walk in the way of their righteous parents. Having one parent of one kind and one of another undermines this purpose which we will look at more in the next section. The particular applications of this for Israel were treaties and intermarriage with the surrounding nations who would lead Israel astray.[27] This is why this issue is given prominence in the narratives of Abraham and Isaac:

> "Put your hand under my thigh, that I may make you swear by the Lord, the God of heaven and God of the earth, that you will not take a wife for my son from the daughters of the Canaanites, among whom I dwell . . . " (Gen 24:2–4)

> "When Esau was forty years old, he took Judith the daughter of Beeri the Hittite to be his wife; and Basemath the daughter of Elon the Hittite, and they made life bitter for Isaac and Rebekah . . . Then Rebekah said to Isaac, 'I loathe my life because of the Hittite women. If Jacob marries one of the Hittite women like these, one of the women of the land, what good will my life be to me?' Then Isaac called Jacob and blessed him and directed him, 'You must not take a wife from the Canaanite women.'" (Gen 26:34–35; 27:46—28:1)

The same truth is applied to the daughters of Israel through God's intention that Sarah and Rebekah have no union with foreign men.[28] This principle of God's people avoiding fellowship and partnership with outsiders is reaffirmed in the New Testament:

> "Do not be unequally yoked with unbelievers. For what partnership has righteousness with lawlessness? Or what fellowship has light with darkness? What accord has Christ with Belial? Or what portion does a believer share with an unbeliever?" (2 Cor 6:15)

> "Therefore do not become partners with them; for at one time you were darkness but now you are light in the Lord. Walk as children

---

26. Just as Eve and Sarah led their husbands astray—in Sarah's case by persuading Abraham to get her a son by sleeping with her maid Hagar. If these wives of good origin can so lead their husbands astray, then the situation will be far worse with foreign wives—foreign in the sense of their character and standards rather than their ethnicity as such.
27. See, e.g., Numbers 25:1–3; Deuteronomy 7:1–5.
28. Genesis 12:10–20; 20:1–17; 26:6–11.

of light (for the fruit of light is found in all that is good and right and true) ... Take no part in the unfruitful works of darkness ... " (Eph 5:7–11)

The New Testament also re-affirms that brotherly hatred is a warning sign to look out for, and persecution something to watch for even in our family:

"We should not be like Cain, who was of the evil one and murdered his brother. And why did he murder him? Because his own deeds were evil and his brother's righteous. Do not be surprised, brothers, that the world hates you ... " (1 John 3:12–13)

"I have come to set a man against his father, and a daughter against her mother, and a daughter-in-law against her mother-in-law. A person's enemies will be those of his own household." (Matt 10:35–36)

PROVIDING WIVES FROM WITHIN OUR PEOPLE

This reality of different kinds raised a problem for Abraham and his offspring. Although God had promised to bless Abraham and Isaac with numerous offspring, the field of suitable wives seemed almost impossibly small. Abraham and Rebekah must find wives for their sons from among their own folk, rather than among the "daughters from the land" around them, the daughters of the Canaanites and Hittites.[29]

In Moses' time also, Israelite men were looking further afield than their own people for a wife, and were being led astray as a result.[30] Yet the history of God's people is filled with stories of his almost miraculous provision of good spouses from within his people, to those who refuse what is readily available and rely on God to provide. This was the case for both Abraham and Rebekah, so it's no surprise that it's the central message for God's people in the story of the creation of Eve, in the following way.

In Genesis 2, among all the animals who are made "from the ground" (and which symbolize the nations that surround God's people)[31] no suitable companion is found for Adam. Accordingly, Eve is not made "from

---

29. Genesis 24:3; 27:46.
30. Numbers 31:15–16. See also Deuteronomy 7:3–4.
31. As we saw in chapter 4.

the ground," but is specially provided from within Adam himself. We see in Adam's response both his marveling that God could provide Eve from within him, and also that he had to wait some time for God to provide her: "This *at last* is bone of *my* bones and flesh of *my* flesh; she shall be called Woman, because she was taken out of Man" (Gen 2:23).

So believers don't need to go roving outside of God's people to find companionship. Even when things look bleak, God will provide from surprisingly close to home. For Moses there was given his brother Aaron, David was given his persecutor Saul's son Jonathan, Jeremiah was not without helpers and faithful companions in the midst of widespread apostasy, and God raised up a number of fellow Galileans to be Jesus' disciples and companions.

LIFE AND LESSONS FROM DUST AND DEADNESS

Another problem for God's promise of offspring was that Sarah, Rebekah, Leah, and Rachel were all initially barren. It might seem pointless and hard that God should promise offspring so long before he was going to provide it, but one of the things God wanted to do was to grow Abraham's faith that God's word was sufficient to provide new life from within the midst of human deadness:

> " . . . in the presence of the God in whom he believed, who gives life to the dead and calls into existence the things that do not exist. In hope he believed against hope, that he should become the father of many nations, as he had been told, 'So shall your offspring be.' He did not weaken in faith when he considered his own body, which was as good as dead (since he was about a hundred years old), or when he considered the deadness of Sarah's womb. No unbelief made him waver concerning the promise of God, but he grew strong in his faith as he gave glory to God, fully convinced that God was able to do what he had promised." (Rom 4:17–21)

For Abraham to gain this faith the promised child had to come from Abraham and Sarah's own dead bodies rather than from outside.[32] Also, God promised offspring to Abraham on four separate occasions before he fulfilled it[33] in order to emphasize that the means of this new life—the true source of Isaac and all the other offspring that would come—was the

---

32. Genesis 15:4; 17:16–21.
33. Genesis 12:2; 15:4; 17:6, 19; 18:10.

spoken word of God. Accordingly, Paul distinguishes Isaac (and all believers) from Ishmael on the basis that Isaac was a child of the promise while Ishmael was born according to the flesh,[34] even though both were born through the usual physical processes.

This is similar to the key promise of Deuteronomy that God would bring new life from within Israel, precisely when both their hearts and their situation as a body of people were most devoid of life and earthly hope:[35]

> "And when all these things come upon you, the blessing and the curse, which I have set before you, and you call them to mind among all the nations where the LORD your God has driven you ... then the LORD your God will restore your fortunes and have mercy on you again, and he will gather you from all the peoples where the LORD your God has scattered you ... And he will make you more prosperous and numerous than your fathers. And the LORD your God will circumcise your heart and the heart of your offspring, so that you will love the LORD your God with all your heart and with all your soul, that you may live." (Deut 30:1–6)

So the origins of national Israel in Genesis are a lesson about God's purpose of bringing life to the deadness of their hearts and hopes. The centrality of this purpose for Israel was recognized by the prophets:

> "Like a pregnant woman who writhes and cries out in her pangs when she is near to giving birth, so were we because of you, O LORD; we were pregnant, we writhed, but we have given birth to wind. We have accomplished no deliverance in the earth, and the inhabitants of the world have not fallen. Your dead shall live; their bodies shall rise. You who dwell in the dust, awake and sing for joy! For your dew is a dew of light, and the earth will give birth to the dead." (Isa 26:17–19)

> "For as the earth brings forth its sprouts, and as a garden causes what is sown in it to sprout up, so the LORD God will cause righteousness and praise to sprout up before all nations. For Zion's sake I will not keep silent, and for Jerusalem's sake I will not be quiet, until her righteousness goes forth as brightness, and her salvation as a burning torch. The nations shall see your righteousness ... For

---

34. Galatians 4:23, 28.

35. It's also no coincidence that Luke's gospel begins with barren Elizabeth waiting for a son (Luke 1:5–8), oppressed Israel waiting for a savior (Luke 1:54–55, 68–79), God announcing that a child and a savior will come (Luke 1:13–17), and they come.

as a young man marries a young woman, so shall your sons marry you." (Isa 61:11—62:5)

"Then he said to me, 'Prophesy over these bones, and say to them, O dry bones, hear the word of the LORD. Thus says the Lord GOD to these bones: Behold, I will cause breath [or Spirit] to enter you, and you shall live . . . these bones are the whole house of Israel. Behold, they say, 'Our bones are dried up, and our hope is lost; we are indeed cut off.' Therefore prophesy, and say to them, Thus says the LORD: Behold, I will open your graves and raise you from your graves, O my people. And I will bring you into the land of Israel . . . And I will put my Spirit within you, and you shall live, and I will place you in your own land." (Ezek 37:4–14)

A notable thing about all of these passages is that they use ideas and images that hark back not just to Abraham and Sarah, but right back to Genesis 1 where God calls plant, animal, and human life into existence from the lifeless earth by his spoken word,[36] with the unspoken promise that they will all be fruitful and multiply, and where God blesses Adam such that he will multiply to become the father of all nations.[37] So the Genesis 1 portrayal of God calling life from the dust seems to be a lesson of how he will bring life to a spiritually barren Israel, through a righteous remnant. The parable of the sower conveys a similar truth: the word of God is like seed in good earth that brings abundant spiritual offspring to the righteous. But what makes this earth good, these people righteous, so that all spiritual hardness and weeds have been removed?

IMPROVING NATURE BY PLOWING AND PRUNING

I still remember the magic and excitement of reading a copy of *The One Straw Revolution* loaned to me by a neighbor. In this book Masanobu Fukuoka, a Japanese farmer and plant scientist, details his journey in philosophy and farming, and his consequent practice of seeking to understand, work with, and be subordinate to nature rather than imposing and intervening by plowing and pruning to get the food and the beauty that we want. Even if his book has not been widely read, it has probably been a significant part of the drift away from what some might call a biblical outlook (but

---

36. Genesis 1:11, 24; 2:19. The phrase "And God said" is perhaps the most repeated of all phrases in Genesis 1.
37. Acts 17:26.

is really just an Ancient Near Eastern and even more widespread human outlook) on nature and "wilderness." Many countries now have reserves of natural environment where human intervention is kept to a minimum, along with legislation that protects wild plants and animals.[38]

This shift in thinking about the natural environment has been paralleled by a more positive assessment of human nature and therefore of letting nature take its course with our children—albeit with some gentle guidance and nurture—rather than cutting out and curbing unruly behavior and growth. Even in schools where discipline and control have now become dominating realities, there is an aversion to using physical pain to curb unruly behavior, and a heavy reliance on "Everyone gets a trophy." Circumcision is widely seen as an utterly pointless medical procedure. Even among believers, bringing up children "in the discipline and instruction of the Lord" is often reduced to little more than teaching basic doctrines that are disconnected from conduct. The children of Christian leaders are often notorious, and not just because their parents are busy shepherding others.

It raises the question of whether our human nature is in the same boat as the rest of nature. What does Genesis say? In the previous chapter we looked at how God's purpose is to transform our earthly nature to be like his own, and in this section I want to show how Genesis uses nature and our natural tendency to curb and order it for our own purposes, to teach about our own nature and how God's goal for it will be achieved.

One of the larger pictures in Genesis 1–2 is that although God brings plant and animal life from the earth, man must order and improve it. His first given task is to subdue and have dominion over the animals and get them to live peaceably with each other,[39] given that many are carnivores, and many even of the herbivores are bossy.[40] Otherwise, if the animals are all in such harmony from the beginning, one wonders why man is needed to subdue and have dominion over them. Accordingly, Isaiah's end-time picture of carnivores becoming herbivores and becoming friends with them,[41] attributes this achievement to the Messianic youth of Isaiah 11.[42] Noah is a step along the way to the Messiah in that he seems to have taken

---

38. Fukuoka's more important goal of spreading his natural farming method has unfortunately been less catching.
39. Genesis 1:28.
40. We had a particularly bossy nanny goat.
41. Isaiah 65:17, 25.
42. See the discussion in chapter 5.

no extra animals on board to feed the carnivores, so he must have fed them plant-based food.[43] So notwithstanding that the world was very good and without sin in the beginning, it was still only a beginning as far as God was concerned.

God also caused the earth to sprout vegetation and fruit trees,[44] yet there is a sense that God's purposes are not yet fulfilled because "there was no man to work the ground,"[45] and man is also needed to work and keep God's garden of fruit trees.[46] To the Ancient Near Eastern mind this would mean pruning and training the growth of these trees.[47] So again, what comes from the ground needs man to improve it. A key point that Genesis wants us to understand is that not only is man also made from the ground, but that this earthly origin is an essential part of his nature: "Then the LORD God formed the man [Heb. 'adam] of dust from the ground [Heb. 'adamah]" (Gen 2:7).

This is a strong hint that our human nature will, like the animals, the ground and the fruit trees, require subduing, cultivating, pruning, and training, in order to fulfil God's purpose for man that we looked at in the previous chapter. Isaiah and Jeremiah confirm this hint:

> "And now I will tell you what I will do to my vineyard. I will remove its hedge, and it shall be devoured. I will break down its wall, and it shall be trampled down. I will make it a waste. It shall not be pruned or hoed, and briers and thorns shall grow up. I will also command the clouds that they rain no rain upon it.[48] For the vineyard of the LORD of hosts is the house of Israel, and the men of Judah are his pleasant planting; and he looked for justice, but behold, bloodshed; for righteousness, but behold, an outcry!" (Isa 5:5–7)

> "Break up your fallow ground, and sow not among thorns. Circumcise yourselves to the LORD; remove the foreskin of your hearts . . . lest my wrath go forth like fire, and burn with none to quench it, because of the evil of your deeds." (Jer 4:3–4)

---

43. In chapter 1 we looked at problems with the view that Genesis indicates there were no carnivores in the beginning.
44. Genesis 1:11; 2:9.
45. Genesis 2:5.
46. Genesis 2:15.
47. Amos 7:14; Micah 4:3; John 15:2.
48. Possibly alluding to Genesis 2:5.

Here, breaking up fallow ground is equivalent to not sowing among thorns, just as circumcising oneself to the Lord is the same as removing the foreskin of one's heart. So when the parable of the sower speaks of seed sown among thorns, rocks, and hard ground, it's referring to ground that hasn't been plowed. Like Genesis, the parable of the sower compares people and their hearts to soil that God has appointed a man ("the sower") to get a harvest from. Again it's only the cultivated earth that bears fruit—the person whose hardness, superficiality, and worldly ambitions have been broken and rooted up so that they can receive the word of God, as James says:

> "The anger of man does not produce the righteousness of God. Therefore put away all filthiness and rampant wickedness and receive with meekness the implanted word, which is able to save your souls." (Jas 1:20–21)

This need for teaching and training so that we don't become like unruly animals, fruit trees, or fields, is later confirmed in Genesis by the moral deterioration from Adam through Cain to Lamech, the complete deterioration of man prior to the Flood, and God's conclusion after the Flood that "the intention of man's heart is evil from his youth."[49] So a key reason why Abraham represents a turning point in Genesis is that in him God has begun the process of teaching and training humanity in his righteous ways:

> "For I have chosen him, that he may command his children and his household after him to keep the way of the Lord by doing righteousness and justice, so that the Lord may bring to Abraham what he has promised him." (Gen 18:19)

The *Shema*, the heart of God's covenant requirement for Israel, confirms the importance of this purpose:

> "Hear, O Israel: The Lord our God, the Lord is one. And you shall love the Lord your God with all your heart and with all your soul and with all your might. And these words that I command you today shall be on your heart. You shall repeat them to your sons, and you shall talk of them when you sit in your house, and when you walk by the way, and when you lie down, and when you rise." (Deut 6:4–7)

This indicates that both teaching and learning God's commands involves wholeheartedness, love. But later on, Deuteronomy testifies that this

---

49. Genesis 8:21.

Seed and Soil that Speak of Salvation

wholehearted love is something that God himself will have to produce in his people, because after an initial time of blessing for righteousness, Israel will indeed rebel and be cursed:

> "And when all these things come upon you, the blessing and the curse which I have set before you, and you call them to mind among all the nations where the Lord your God has driven you, and return to the Lord your God, you and your children . . . the Lord your God will circumcise your heart and the heart of your offspring, so that you will love the Lord your God with all your heart and with all your soul, that you may live." (Deut 30:1–2, 6)

This indicates that it's the hardships which God brings upon Israel that will make the difference, and break up their hardness and root up their idolatry so that they receive God's word. So heart circumcision involves hardship, just as John's reference to being baptized with the Holy Spirit implies suffering.[50] Ezekiel connects this hardship of exile which creates a new heart within Israel, to the cleansing work of the Holy Spirit:

> "I will take you from the nations and gather you from all the countries and bring you into your own land. I will sprinkle clean water on you, and you shall be clean from all your uncleannesses, and from all your idols I will cleanse you. And I will give you a new heart, and a new spirit I will put within you. And I will remove the heart of stone and put within you a heart of flesh. And I will put my Spirit within you, and cause you to walk in my statutes and be careful to obey my rules." (Ezek 36:24–27)

Jesus also connects this heart cleansing by the Holy Spirit, to the pruning or circumcising effect of his commandments:

> "If you love me you will keep my commandments . . . If anyone loves me he will keep my word . . . the Holy Spirit, whom the Father will send in my name, he will teach you all things and bring to remembrance all that I have said to you . . . I am the true vine, and my Father is the vinedresser. Every branch in me that does not bear fruit he takes away, and every branch that does bear fruit he prunes [Greek *kathairei*], that it may bear more fruit. Already you are clean [Greek *katharoi*] because of the word that I have spoken to you." (John 14:15, 23–26; 15:1–3)

Scripture therefore indicates two things about this heart renewal by the Holy Spirit. One is that he works especially through suffering, rather

---

50. Matthew 3:11–12; cf. Isaiah 4:4.

than through hyped up or mystical "worship services" and eloquent or "prophetic" words which are invariably positive. Accordingly it was after Jesus' testing and deprivation of food and fellowship in the wilderness that he "returned in the power of the Holy Spirit to Galilee."[51]

The other thing Scripture indicates is that although the Holy Spirit works through the word he has inspired, the preaching of this word primarily involves rebuking, reproving, correcting, urging, and training in righteousness.[52] While the center of this word is the gospel, the teaching of sound doctrine involves a sharpness that, while not ungracious, still stings like salt as it cuts away uncleanness and rank growth to produce sound conduct:[53]

> "For the grace of God has appeared, bringing salvation for all people, training us to renounce ungodliness and worldly passions, and to live self-controlled, upright, and godly lives in the present age." (Tit 2:11–12)

So God's purpose is that this teaching and discipline spread through all humanity from his people, beginning with Abraham in his household, spreading through Israel via priests, prophets, and parents, then through Jesus in the gospels, his apostles in the epistles, and his disciples (notably pastors, prophets, and parents) from here on.[54]

In conclusion, although governing the natural world doesn't necessarily need to be as interventionist as it was in the Ancient Near East, Moses is happy to plunder the thinking of his time to teach that people at least need the plowing and pruning of suffering to uproot their idols, break up their hardness, and open up their thinking to receive God's word.

But the word of God continues to uproot and prune away whatever is unrighteous if we receive it and make room for it. So there is a kind of suffering that goes with hearing it, because it convicts us of sins and idols we need to get rid of, passions and habits we need to reign in, and it requires us to think, wait, and trust. Again, this is the Holy Spirit's work, but he does it through the word.[55]

---

51. Luke 4:14.

52. Conflating 2 Timothy 3:16 and 4:2.

53. Titus 2; Hebrews 4:12; Revelation 19:13–15. Colossians 4:6 uses the salt metaphor to teach that while our words need to be gracious, this will involve being savory rather than sweet.

54. Matthew 28:19–20; Ephesians 6:4.

55. So the convicting work of the Spirit mentioned in John 16:8 follows on from Jesus

Accordingly, circumcision was given together with the requirement that Abraham keep God's ways and get his household and offspring to do the same.[56] As Calvin says, "For the Jews, circumcision was the symbol by which they were admonished that whatever comes forth from man's seed, that is, the whole nature of mankind, is corrupt and needs pruning."[57]

More importantly, circumcision signifies the pruning effect on human hearts, of the living and active teaching of God's ways from his word. So while we are indeed to ask for the Holy Spirit to renew our minds, we mustn't neglect our responsibility of acquiring and understanding the word for ourselves, sowing it in the hearts of ourselves and others.

SACRIFICING OR SAVING OUR SEED

Circumcision might help us accept the need to prune the unruly growth of ungodliness in our children—but what if a son refused to obey?

> "If a man has a stubborn and rebellious son who will not obey the voice of his father or mother and, though they discipline him, will not listen to them, then his father and his mother shall take hold of him and bring him to the elders of his city at the gate of the place where he lives, and they shall say to the elders of his city, 'This our son is stubborn and rebellious; he will not obey our voice; he is a glutton and a drunkard.' Then all the men of the city shall stone him to death with stones. So you shall purge the evil from your midst, and all Israel shall hear and fear." (Deut 21:18–21)

This complete removal of the ungodly from the body of God's people was the more prominent significance of circumcision, and this is indicated in several ways when circumcision was first given. One of these is God's opening words: "I am God almighty: walk before me and be blameless, that I may make my covenant between me and you, and may multiply you greatly" (Gen 17:1–2). So God will tolerate no departures or deviations from his ways. After giving the requirement of circumcision he adds, "Any uncircumcised male who is not circumcised in the flesh of his foreskin shall be cut off from his people; he has broken my covenant" (Gen 17:14).

Finally, in the next chapter God decides to tell Abraham what he is about to do to Sodom and Gomorrah, because,

---

telling about the pruning and cleansing effect of his words in John 15.

56. Genesis 17:1, 10–14; 18:19.

57. Calvin, *Institutes*, IV.XIV.21.

> "I have chosen him, that he may command his children and his household after him to keep the way of the Lord by doing righteousness and justice, so that the Lord may bring to Abraham what he has promised him." (Gen 18:19)

That is, Abraham and his children and household need to know how God removes the wicked from his land and his presence, so that Abraham will be zealous to remove unrighteousness and injustice from his own children and household, so that his offspring will indeed be blessed.

When these things are viewed together, they indicate that circumcision especially signifies the removal of the disobedient and ungodly from God's land and his people. But the question is left open as to who is responsible for doing it. God removes Sodom and Gomorrah, but Abraham must command and enforce God's commandments upon his children. We see a similar situation in the Exodus and the Conquest. Sometimes Israel removed the disobedient from among them, as with a Sabbath-breaker.[58] At other times God removed the ungodly, as with the plague on those who complained about meat,[59] and as with Korah and his associates.[60] Sometimes God and Israel both played parts as with the idolaters in the golden calf incident,[61] and with Achan at Jericho.[62]

Ultimately Israel was responsible to remove the disobedient from its land and people, but God would sometimes do it himself if his people failed to, as happened with the sons of Eli and with David's son Absalom.[63] This was a foretaste of the fact that Israel as a whole would fail to remove the disobedient from among them, so that in the end God would remove them as a nation from the land.

The key problem is that we are naturally reluctant to allow issues of truth, righteousness, and justice to be given higher priority than fellowship or at least friendly relations with our children (or our friends or parents). As Professor Dumbledore said in *Harry Potter and the Philosopher's Stone*, "It takes a great deal of bravery to stand up to your enemies, but a great deal

---

58. Numbers 15:32–36.
59. Numbers 11.
60. Numbers 16.
61. Exodus 32:25–29, 35.
62. Joshua 7.
63. 1 Samuel 2–4; 2 Samuel 17:14 18:5. David also failed to act either when his eldest son Amnon raped Absalom's sister Tamar and then refused to marry her, or when Absalom afterward had him murdered.

Seed and Soil that Speak of Salvation

more to stand up to your friends,"[64] because we don't want to lose them. It's a crucial reason why Israel's morality might degenerate to the point of Exile. If Eli the priest and David the king were both guilty of not taking decisive action when they needed to, how much worse would the problem be among the less righteous majority that they led?

So Moses draws attention to this problem in Genesis. One way he does this is by consistently portraying both the desire of mothers to have sons and the grief they give, whether by doing wrong or by being taken away. Cain and Abel are portrayed as the two archetypes here. Eve is initially triumphant and satisfied with having "gained (Heb. *Qānah*) a man," and so she calls his name Cain (Heb. *qayin*).[65] Genesis then says that she added (Heb. *toseph*) his brother Abel, whose name means "breath" or "vapor."[66] This referred to the fact that Abel wouldn't be around for long, and would soon be just a memory. Righteous Abel is killed and Cain is cursed from the land and leaves it, just as Israel increasingly murdered the righteous prophets prior to the Exile.

So Cain is also taken away from Eve both in relational terms because of what he did, and because he leaves the land of his home. Cain represents the son who is gained but is really a loss, not just because he murders righteous Abel, but because his descendants are in some ways even further degenerated. Eve's experience is echoed by that of both Rebekah and Rachel. Like Cain, Esau wants to kill Jacob, and like Cain's descendant Lamech, he marries two wives (and another one later).[67] Similar to Abel, Rebekah's favorite son Jacob has to be sent away, and is gone for about twenty years. So again, Rebekah faces the loss of both her sons:

> "Behold, your brother Esau comforts himself about you by planning to kill you. Now therefore, my son, obey my voice. Arise, flee to Laban my brother in Haran and stay with him a while, until your brother's fury turns away . . . Why should I be bereft of you both in one day?" (Gen 27:42–25)

Even though Rebekah isn't bereft of Jacob by death, she still loses him by distance. She also feels that Esau murdering Jacob would be the final

---

64. Heyman & Columbus, *Harry Potter and the Philosopher's Stone*.

65. Genesis 4:1.

66. Heb. *habel*, which shares the same root as *hebel* in Ecclesiastes ("breath/vanity/meaningless").

67. Wenham notes that one of Lamech's wives has the same name as one of Esau's wives (Gen 1–15, 112).

relational loss of Esau, but like Eve she loses him by distance anyway as he ends up moving to Seir, not least because he is more restless in his homeland than Jacob:[68] more of a wanderer like Cain.

Rachel's desire for sons is similar to that of Eve: "She said to Jacob, 'Give me sons or I will die... And she called his name Joseph (Heb. *yoseph*), saying, 'May the LORD add to me another son'" (Gen 30:1, 24). So we see the "adding" verb (Heb. *yasaph*) that was used to refer to a second son for Eve, now underlined with reference to a second son for Rachel also. Yet this second son is also a source of grief because he makes Rachel's own life a mere breath in the narrative and she doesn't get to enjoy either him or her triumph regarding Leah. So she calls him "Son of my Sorrow" as she is dying.[69]

Sarah is also happy to merely obtain children regardless of what God's purposes or promises may be,[70] but once again Ishmael gives her grief, both in causing Hagar to look with contempt on Sarah, and then when Ishmael makes sport of Isaac.[71] Lot's daughters show even less regard for God's purposes and provision in their own priority and method of obtaining sons.[72] So although God's curse in Genesis 3 refers to a woman's pain in giving birth, it's really pointing to the grief that goes with women trying to get sons merely for their own sake. Mary's heart would also be pierced with grief for her firstborn son,[73] and perhaps not only at his death, but because she would lose possession of him in a relational sense: he wouldn't be her "baby" for long.[74]

Similarly, Genesis portrays fathers as reluctant to give up or jeopardize their beloved sons, and it portrays God as consistently causing it and requiring it. Abraham is reluctant to send Ishmael away but God requires it.[75] Genesis 37 portrays Jacob's love for Joseph, his keeping Joseph at home while his other sons are afield with the livestock, and how God takes Joseph away from Jacob. Judah is afraid for his youngest son Shelah so he avoids

---

68. Genesis 25:27.
69. Genesis 35:18. See also Wenham, *Genesis 16–50*, 326.
70. Genesis 16.
71. Genesis 16:4–5; 20:9–10.
72. Genesis 19:30–38.
73. Luke 2:34–35.
74. Luke 2:46–51; John 2:4; 19:26–27.
75. Genesis 21:9–12.

Seed and Soil that Speak of Salvation

giving Tamar to him, but is brought to admit his fault in the end.[76] Finally, Joseph is just as displeased that his older son receives the lesser blessing, as Abraham is that his older son Ishmael must be sent away.[77] This brings us to what I and probably many others think is the very center and climax of Genesis (though it has a few such climaxes), which is where God requires Abraham to give up his beloved son Isaac, and Abraham obeys.

So God didn't just require Israel to give up their disobedient and ungodly children: he required all of them to give up their firstborn son (though he allowed them to be redeemed).[78] Why? Firstly, because God's ultimate purpose is to take our offspring to be his own special possession, as with Israel:

> "If you will indeed obey my voice and keep my covenant, you shall be my treasured possession among all peoples." (Exod 19:5)

> "Then you shall say to Pharaoh, 'Thus says the LORD, "Israel is my firstborn son, and I say to you, let my son go that he may serve me. If you refuse to let him go, behold, I will kill your firstborn son."'" (Exod 4:22–24)

The reason why the redemption of the firstborn is so closely tied to the Passover[79] was because Israel had to learn the same lesson as Pharaoh: that God wants to take our children for himself, to serve him, as Hannah recognized.[80] Likewise God took Adam and brought him to serve in God's garden,[81] and he took Enoch simply to have him with him.

In requiring us to sacrifice our offspring, God merely wants us learn his own ways, as he would ultimately send away and give up his own son. We can't receive God's blessing of fruitfulness on our offspring while ever we are grasping of it. So Genesis provides the background to Jesus' statements that;

> "Unless a grain of wheat falls into the earth and dies, it remains alone; but if it dies it bears much fruit." (John 12:24)

---

76. Genesis 38, notably verse 26.
77. Wenham (Gen 16–50, 466) points out that the same phrase is used in both passages, and implies powerful anger.
78. Exodus 13:1–2, 11–16.
79. Exodus 13:1–2, 11–16.
80. 1 Samuel 1.
81. The same "serving" word is used here in Genesis 2:15 as in Exodus 4:23.

"Everyone who has left houses or brothers or sisters or father or mother or children or lands, for my name's sake, will receive a hundredfold..." (Matt 19:29)

Circumcision provides a second reason why God is this way: as in circumcision where a small part of the body perceived as unclean is removed to make the rest of the body pure, so also Christ became sin and was cut off to purify the rest of the body of God's people.[82] So we need to not be grasping onto friends, family, and fellowship, whether this involves accepting when God has claimed them for himself (such as in death or in serving him away from us), or whether it involves correcting, disciplining, or avoiding them.[83] It's always a heavy business, but as with the removal of Ananias and Sapphira it brings God's blessing of fruitfulness.[84]

SEED THAT GROWS INTO GREATER THINGS, GRADUALLY

Although a seed may appear small and nondescript, it contains everything needed to grow even a huge and majestic tree all by itself. One merely has to plant it in the soil of its native climate, and leave it. It may lie for a long time doing nothing, but the life within has not died, and awaits the right conditions to sprout and grow. More than any other book in Scripture, Genesis portrays the word of God as a seed that gradually unfolds its true meaning and fulfillment and bears fruit, in the following way.

The dominating phrase in Genesis 1 is "And God said..." Initially his spoken word generates things that appear simple on the surface, like the various features of the physical world, and a blessing on mankind such that we are physically filling the earth and ruling it. In Genesis 3, God's curse generates physical pain in childbirth, physical death, a reptile's low-slung bearing, and troubled relations between people and dangerous reptiles, and between husbands and wives.

But we've seen that these physical realities that God's word generates, gradually unfold through Genesis into greater realities. Yet apart from the creation week where physical results are portrayed as following

---

82. Colossians 2:11, where the circumcision of Christ refers to his crucifixion (see O'Brien, *Colossians, Philemon*, 115–16). See also 2 Corinthians 5:21; Ephesians 5:25–27; Isaiah 53:10–11.

83. Matthew 18:15–20.

84. Acts 5:1–14.

Seed and Soil that Speak of Salvation

immediately, God's word often lies dormant for a while before these greater things begin to happen.

For example, although God promises that the seed of the woman will ultimately triumph over the seed of the serpent, it's initially sin rather than righteousness that seems to spread and deepen, as we read of Cain murdering righteous Abel and his descendants degrading further. Yet at the end of this dark chapter we are given a sign that God's promise has not died, and its fulfillment has begun:

> "Adam knew his wife again, and she bore a son and called his name Seth, for she said, "God has appointed for me another offspring in place of Abel, for Cain killed him. To Seth also a son was born, and he called his name Enosh [which means "man/human"]. At that time people began to call upon the name of the LORD." (Gen 4:25-26)

Also, while God promises Abraham a multitude of offspring, his word lies dormant for twenty five years before finding fruition in just one son. Even when Abraham's physical offspring through Jacob have greatly multiplied, they are nearly wiped out in the Exile before the true fulfillment of believers in Christ from every nation, really gets going.[85]

We have also seen how Genesis likes to portray God as bringing life from the earth by his word alone, and this is probably a part of Jesus' precedent for likening the word of God to seed in the parable of the sower. Jesus may be hinting that God's word can lie dormant for a long time before the right conditions make it sprout and germinate. Like his parables, the meaning of particular Scriptures may have to wait for particular life experiences before it begins to open up and reveal and produce the realities it speaks of. This is why "Mary treasured up all these things" spoken about Jesus or by him, "pondering them in her heart."[86]

This is not to say that the word of God always has a mystical meaning for our imagination to discover with the claimed help of the Spirit. Both Jesus and Paul are at pains to make clear that what was hidden and spoken of in parables has now fully unfolded in the apostles' teaching about Jesus. So because the word of God begins as seed, it must be understood as unfolding towards Christ, rather than being read through some Western lens of science or Eastern lens of personal mysticism. It also means that when the word of God starts sprouting and growing in a person, it will grow that

---

85. Isaiah 1:9; 6:11-13; Jeremiah 52:28-30.
86. Luke 2:19, 51.

person towards Christ in terms of character, moving us to purify and prune away what is unrighteous:

> "Having purified your souls by your obedience to the truth for a sincere brotherly love, love one another earnestly from a pure heart, since you have been born anew, not of perishable seed but of imperishable, through the living and abiding word of God; for
> 'All flesh is like grass and all its glory like the flower of grass. The grass withers and the flower falls, but the word of the Lord remains forever.'
> And this word is the gospel that was preached to you. So put away all malice and all deceit and hypocrisy and envy and all slander. Like newborn infants long for the pure spiritual milk, that by it you may grow up into salvation—if indeed you have tasted that the Lord is good." (1 Pet 1:22—2:3)

This is why the fruit of good doctrine is godliness, especially brotherly love. Our slow growth in godliness is a testimony to the slow unfolding of the word in our hearts, not least because they are so hard and stubborn! So because the seed of God's word has fully grown and unfolded in Christ, prophecy is no longer about any new revelation other than the gospel, and this is the great framework that John gives us for understanding Revelation:

> "The revelation of Jesus Christ, which God gave him to show to his servants the things that must soon take place. He made it known by sending his angel to his servant John, *who bore witness to the word of God and to the testimony of Jesus,* even to all that he saw" (Rev 1:1-2).

So John's visions equate to the word of God and the testimony of Jesus. Yet John tells us that he was already in exile for testifying to these same things:

> "I, John ... was on the island called Patmos on account of the word of God and the testimony of Jesus. I was in the Spirit on the Lord's day, and I heard behind me a loud voice like a trumpet saying, 'Write what you see in a book and send it to the seven churches ...'" (Rev 1:9-10)

So in a sense John is revealing nothing new in his book. What the book of Revelation does is to bring together and integrate a myriad of Old Testament themes and allusions into a gospel framework—in other words showing how they are fulfilled in Christ—just as Christ did in his own teaching. For prophets, there is nothing more than Christ to reveal:

Seed and Soil that Speak of Salvation

>"'I am a fellow servant with you and your brothers who hold to the testimony of Jesus. Worship God. For the testimony of Jesus is the spirit of prophecy.' Then I saw heaven opened, and behold, a white horse! The one sitting on it is called Faithful and True . . . and the name by which he is called is the Word of God." (Rev 19:10–13)

So "the testimony of Jesus and the word of God" refer to the same reality in Revelation, because once again Jesus and the gospel about him is the full unfolding of all Scripture, its true content. So John's conclusion in Revelation does not reflect an inflated view of the content of his book as opposed to all other Scripture, but rather that a) there is nothing more to add to God's revelation, therefore any prophet who attempts to do so is cursed; and b) the prophetic role of bringing people back to what has already been revealed, continues, so any prophet who covers over things that have been revealed in Jesus (like wrongs and corruptions we need to get rid of) is cursed:

>"I warn everyone who hears the words of the prophecy of this book: if anyone adds to them, God will add to him the plagues described in this book, and if anyone takes away from the words of the book of this prophecy, God will take away his share in the tree of life and in the holy city, which are described in this book." (Rev 22:18–19)

So when people look to new prophetic revelations for guidance and growth, the preaching and understanding of the gospel are correspondingly weak, and godliness is compromised. Prophets should be bringing people back to the new covenant, as the Old Testament prophets continually brought people back to the Sinai covenant. Perhaps a reason for this looking elsewhere than the word for guidance and growth, is that people become impatient with the slowness of the word to unfold in our hearts: we want quicker answers and growth, without having to test our thinking or probe our motives too thoroughly. And while the word (like seed) seems to unfold slowly in our lives, our desperate and deceptive hearts duck, dodge, and delay its penetrating roots even more.

THE SEED OF THE WORD THAT IS FOOD FOR THE SOUL

Early Genesis also indicates that the word of God shares another quality with seed, namely that they both contain nourishment for life. If we remember that the essential content of Genesis and Deuteronomy was initially written by the same hand for the same people, we might notice some parallels in the following two passages, one from Genesis and the other from Deuteronomy:

> "... multiply and fill the earth [Heb. *'eretz*] and subdue it ... I have given you every [Heb. *kol*] plant yielding seed that is on the face of all [Heb. *kol*] the earth, and every [Heb. *kol*] tree with seed in its fruit. You shall have them for food." (Gen 1:28–29)

> "The whole [Heb. *kol*] commandment that I command you today you shall be careful to do, that you may live and multiply, and go in and possess the land [Heb. *'eretz*] that the Lord swore to give to your fathers. And you shall remember the whole [Heb. *kol*] way that the Lord your God has led you these forty years ... he humbled you and let you hunger and fed you with manna ... that he might make you know that man does not live by bread alone, but man lives by everything [Heb. *kol*] that comes from the mouth of God." (Deut 8:1–3)

Moses seems to be drawing a parallel here between seed in Genesis and the commands of God in Deuteronomy. Another parallel that supports this picture is that in Genesis 1, seed is God's special gift to man so that he may flourish relative to the animals, as the Israelites in Egypt prospered and multiplied relative to their Egyptian neighbors because Joseph provided them with food. But God's special provision to Israel so that they may prosper relative to their neighboring nations, is his word:

> "He declares his word to Jacob, his statutes and rules to Israel. He has not dealt thus with any other nation; they do not know his rules. (Ps 147:19–20)

> "See, I have taught you statutes and rules, as the Lord my God commanded me, so that you will do them in the land that you are entering to take possession of it. Keep them and do them, for that will be your wisdom and your understanding in the sight of the peoples, who, when they hear all these statutes, will say, 'Surely this great nation is a wise and understanding people.'" (Deut 4:5–6)

Moses and the psalmist are not talking here about the power of God's promises or actions to sustain or grow our faith. They are talking about God's commands and the life that comes through keeping them. This life comes not merely through avoiding God's curse for disobedience, but especially because when we obey God's commands in faith he reveals to us how good they are, and they become our life and we delight in his wisdom, as in Psalm 19 and 119:

> "The law of the LORD is perfect, reviving the soul; the testimony of the LORD is sure, making wise the simple; the precepts of the LORD are right, rejoicing the heart." (Ps 19:7–8)

> "Your testimonies are my delight; they are my counsellors . . . how I love your law! It is my meditation all the day. Your commandment makes me wiser than my enemies . . . How sweet are your words to my taste, sweeter than honey to my mouth! Through your precepts I get understanding; therefore I hate every false way." (Ps 119:24, 97–98, 103–104)

Even in the New Testament Paul can speak of the Law as being "holy and righteous and good,"[87] and of how we come to discover its perfection and goodness when we put it to the test by doing it.[88] Yet this glorying in the righteousness and goodness of God's commands is hard to find in church worship and devotional material today, perhaps partly because although we don't want God to test our hearts, we don't want to test his commands either, and find out if they really are good. We want an untested relationship.

UNDERSTANDING GENESIS, USING SCIENCE, AND WINNING PEOPLE

Jesus' parables may have been creative, but their greater value is their faithful and simple distillation of Scripture, as here with the seed and soil themes in Genesis.

Genesis 1 is likewise a parable of God's goal for this world, a thematic table of contents for Genesis and all of Scripture, which has as its climax a man who is the image of the holy God and lord of the nations, who will multiply into a multitude and so fill the earth with holiness. Then all will be complete and God will rest. The end of Genesis is well along this path, with righteous Joseph the "fruitful branch"[89] as lord of Egypt, and his children who have been blessed to multiply.[90]

---

87. Romans 7:12.
88. Romans 12:2.
89. Genesis 49:22.
90. Genesis 48:14–16, 19.

A key resource that early Genesis uses to tell these parables is natural phenomena that lend themselves rather well to the task, and at many different levels. That is, the references to seed in Genesis 1–2 can refer to different things at the same time, because we are not dealing there with mere allegories where there is only one-on-one correspondence.

So although we said earlier that the natural world and its science can't reveal the hidden realm of God that undergirds and directs it, yet it does provide pointers toward it, and scientists continue to point these out. For example, John Baumgardner and Jeremy Lyon show how both the natural and human worlds depend for their existence on language—whether the language of mathematics that determines how different kinds of matter and energy relate to each other; the language of genetics that determines the meanings of DNA code; the computer programming languages we increasingly rely on; and human language, the creative dynamic of human existence which God crippled at Babel in Genesis 11.[91] This is similar to Genesis 1, where God shapes matter by speaking to it.

Baumgardner and Lyon also show how language and meaning are themselves immaterial, and exist independently of the physical things that they govern, which is similar to Hebrews 11:3—" . . . what is seen was not made out of things that are visible."[92] Finally, they show how mathematics does indeed possess the two components that comprise language: assigning meaning to otherwise meaningless symbols to form a vocabulary of "words," and a set of rules by which these "words" may be joined together to create more complex messages that carry meaning.[93] So Galileo's famous statement is not just rhetoric: mathematics is indeed the language with which God has written (or spoken) the universe.

This is the way ahead in the creation/evolution debate, just as it was in the past. Creationists can reach out to evolutionists by using the very discoveries that seem to support evolutionary theories to tell truths about the heart of reality, instead of worrying about what scientific ground they may be conceding. For example, all vertebrate embryos have a tail and slits that resemble gills.[94] While the theory that our embryos recapitulate our evolu-

91. Baumgardner & Lyon, "Linguistic Argument," 771–86.
92. Ibid.
93. Ibid.
94. In fact all chordates (a slightly larger group) have these features at some stage in their life, along with at least a rudimentary digestive tract, a rod of cartilage that functions as a spine, and a hollow nerve cord which develops in vertebrates to a central nervous system.

tionary past has been debunked, and while these "primitive" embryonic features are not useless hangovers from the past but vital parts of embryo development, it still shows a biological relationship that we share with each other. The natural and obvious question it raises for anyone who sees these things (whatever their philosophy) is "Are we then biologically related?"

Evolutionists would be a lot less irritated by believers if they would grant the obvious—and we can. There is a Genesis truth and therefore a Gospel truth here that we saw earlier: we are made from the same stuff the animals are made from, because we need to share in their substance to rule them well, just as Jesus had to share in our substance and sufferings. There is another Genesis truth that we focused on in chapter 4: God takes things he has made and transforms them into something new and "higher." While genetics and the fossil record may not give enough support to purely natural evolution on their own, at least there is the option that God took "lower" organisms, at whatever time and sequence is indicated by paleontology, and crafted them into "higher" life forms.

So early Genesis (and God's word generally) can help to shed light on science, though not by interpreting it literally. Also, Genesis provides a great illustration of how natural phenomena can be such apt summaries of the as-yet hidden realm that God is working towards, and of how one can bear witness to it by interacting with people's cultural and intellectual foundations rather than trying to demonize and destroy them.

Chapter 6

Blight and Blessing in Genesis and Deuteronomy

WHILE TRYING TO THINK of a suitable title for this chapter, Gollum's exclamation when he first met Bilbo ("Bless us and splash us!") kept coming into my thoughts.[1] When I decided to think about it I immediately thought of a priest in robes who blesses and sprinkles water on people. This sort of eloquent ritual may be a common perception of how God blesses people, but it falls rather short of what we see unfolding in Genesis and beyond. Gollum's frequent curses prove equally impotent, and again Genesis portrays much weightier and long-term outcomes for the curse of God. This chapter looks at how God's blessing and curse unfold through Genesis and the rest of Scripture, and how they work out in daily life. In fact I want to begin with a recent incident in our own daily life, when my wife rushed inside saying, "Jesus, help us!"

OUR FIRST AMBULANCE CALL-OUT, AND ANOTHER STORY TO REINFORCE THE RULES

It turned out our son had badly injured his hand and wrist while experimenting with ammunition, so it wasn't long before he (and we) were hearing some sobering stories of others who had fared worse from similar ventures. These helped to clarify our newfound appreciation of the goodness of laws

---

1. Tolkien, *The Hobbit*, 68.

that might have seemed strict before, and of the potentially powerful consequences for breaking them.

It was similar when we had someone from a government authority come and give his work safety presentation for the people we were training. Something inside me was dying and something else was violently rising up as I listened to all the requirements and penalties, but when he finished up with some surprising stories of workplace fun gone wrong and safety rules neglected, it gave some bite to what he had been saying.

We might feel a bit the same as we plow through the rules, requirements, and repetition in the book of Deuteronomy, especially when we get to the blessings for obedience and curses for disobedience in chapter 28. But when we compare these blessings and curses with those in Genesis, it suddenly becomes apparent that Genesis fulfills the role of stories that show how keeping or breaking God's laws work out in practice. In fact Deuteronomy points the reader back to Genesis by its frequent comment that God's gift of the land to the multitudes of Israel is itself the outworking of his blessing on Abraham, Isaac, and Jacob.[2]

Genesis likewise points the reader forward to the rules and requirements of Deuteronomy and the other Mosaic books, as in the following example:

> "Sojourn in this land, and I will be with you and will bless you . . . and I will establish the oath that I swore to Abraham your father . . . because Abraham obeyed my voice and kept my charge, my commandments, my statutes, and my laws." (Gen 26:2–5)

The thing is that we don't read of God giving Abraham very many rules to keep. The final part of the excerpt above feels more at home in Deuteronomy,[3] and seems especially intended for the Israelite reader who *had* received God's charge, commandments, statutes, and laws.[4]

So this chapter looks at how God's laws, blessings, and curses in Genesis unfold toward a fulfillment in Deuteronomy and beyond. I have

---

2. E.g., Deuteronomy 1:10–11 (pointing back to God's promised blessing to Abraham); 4:37, 40; 6:10; 7:8–11.

3. E.g., Deuteronomy 6:17, 20; 7:11.

4. Genesis 9:20–27 also reveals how the destruction that is decreed for the Canaanite inhabitants of the land, represents the unfolding of God's curse on their forefathers, just as the sin of their forefathers has unfolded into their own depravity and ripeness for judgement (Genesis 15:16). The Sodom narrative (Gen 18–19), Esau's wives (Gen 26:34–35), and the rape of Dinah (Gen 34) already indicate that things are not good in Canaan.

included a fair bit of material from Deuteronomy and Isaiah, but some may prefer to skim over this and get to the point more quickly.

THE BIG THREE BLESSINGS IN GENESIS AND DEUTERONOMY

Following is a representative sample of the blessings and curses in Deuteronomy 28, in which one may notice the prominence of offspring, dominion or subservience to surrounding nations, and food and farming (the ESV's "shall" has repeatedly been changed to "will"):

> "If you faithfully obey the voice of the LORD your God, being careful to do all his commandments that I command you today, the LORD your God will set you high above all the nations of the earth. And all these blessings will come upon you and overtake you, if you obey the voice of the LORD your God ... Blessed will be the fruit of your womb and the fruit of your ground ... The LORD will cause your enemies who rise against you to be defeated before you. They will come out against you one way and flee before you seven ways ... And he will bless you in the land that the LORD your God is giving you ... And all the peoples of the earth will see that you are called by the name of the LORD, and they will be afraid of you.
>
> And the LORD will make you abound in prosperity, in the fruit of your womb and in the fruit of your livestock and in the fruit of your ground, within the land that the LORD swore to your fathers to give you ... And you will lend to many nations, but you will not borrow. And the LORD will make you the head and not the tail ...
>
> But if you will not obey the voice of the LORD your God or be careful to do all his commandments and his statutes that I command you today, then all these curses will come upon you and overtake you ... Cursed will be the fruit of your womb and the fruit of your ground, the increase of your herds and the young of your flock ...
>
> The LORD will cause you to be defeated before your enemies. You will go out one way against them and flee seven ways before them ... You will carry much seed into the field and gather in little, for the locust will consume it. You will plant vineyards and dress them, but you will neither drink of the wine nor gather the grapes, for the worm will eat them. You will have olive trees throughout all your territory, but you will not anoint yourself with the oil, for your olives will drop off ... Your sons and your daughters will

be given to another people, while your eyes look on and fail with longing for them all day long, but you will be helpless. A nation that you have not known will eat up the fruit of your ground and of all your labors . . . The sojourner who is among you will rise higher and higher above you, and you will come down lower and lower. He will lend to you, and you will not lend to him. He will be the head, and you will be the tail." (Deut 28:1–44)

The blessing on man in Genesis 1 focuses on the same three areas of offspring, dominion, and food and farming:

"God blessed them, and God said to them, "Be fruitful and multiply, fill the earth and subdue it, and have dominion over the fish of the sea and over the birds of the heavens and over every living thing that moves on the earth. Behold, I have given you every plant yielding seed that is on the face of all the earth, and every tree with its seed in its fruit. You shall have them for food." (Gen 1:28–29)

When man disobeys God in Genesis 3, the same three blessings on offspring, dominion, and food are withdrawn:

"I will surely multiply your pain in childbearing; in pain you will bring forth children. Your desire will be for your husband, and he will rule over you. And to Adam he said, 'Because you have listened to the voice of your wife and have eaten of the tree of which I commanded you, 'You shall not eat of it,' cursed is the ground because of you; in pain you will eat from it all the days of your life; thorns and thistles it will bring forth for you, and you will eat the plants of the field. By the sweat of your face you will eat bread . . . " (Gen 3:16–19)

While the withdrawn blessings on offspring and food are clear, the withdrawn blessing of dominion—expressed in the statement that the man will rule over the woman—has taken a slightly different guise because the woman has become a symbol of the people of God. This is how John understands it in the book of Revelation:

"And a great sign appeared in heaven: a woman clothed with the sun, with the moon under her feet, and on her head a crown of twelve stars. She was pregnant and was crying out in birth pains and the agony of giving birth . . . And the dragon stood before the woman who was about to give birth, so that when she bore her child he might devour it. She gave birth to a male child, one who is to rule all the nations with a rod of iron." (Rev 12:1–5)

So the serpent (Hebrew *naḥāsh*) of Genesis 3 is now explicitly identified as a dragon, and the woman is clothed with the sun, moon, and stars of Joseph's kingly dream.[5] But otherwise the essential features are the same as in Genesis 3: the woman represents Israel, and she gives birth painfully to a son who will defeat the dragon. If we remember how Israel was like an adulteress who abandoned her husband (God) to consort with the surrounding nations,[6] then the hint for Israel in Genesis 3:15–16 is that if Israel runs after the gods of other nations, God will hand her over to their dominion.

This makes better sense of Genesis 3:16 than a literal reading. While many commentators have tried to make it sound bad that "Your desire will be for your husband and he will rule over you," the Hebrew words for "desire" and "ruling" are neutral terms: they don't automatically imply dark desire or domineering. Male headship is already implied by the wife helping the husband in Genesis 2:18 and the man naming the woman in Genesis 2:23, just as man has dominion over the animals and also names them. And something is wrong when wives *don't* desire their husbands.

So we have the same three blessings withdrawn for disobedience in both Genesis 3 and Deuteronomy 28.[7] We see the same three blessings reinstated after the Flood:

> "And God blessed Noah and his sons and said to them, 'Be fruitful and multiply and fill the earth. The fear of you and the dread of you shall be upon every beast of the earth . . . Into your hand they are delivered. Every moving thing that lives will be food for you. And as I gave you the green plants, I give you everything.'" (Gen 9:1–3)

So the blessings on food and offspring are back! But the blessing of man's dominion and the animals' servitude is less clear until we come to the blessing on Shem and the curse on Canaan at the end of Genesis 9:

> "When Noah awoke from his wine and knew what his youngest son had done to him, he said, 'Cursed be Canaan; a servant of servants shall he be to his brothers.' He also said, 'Blessed be the Lord, the God of Shem; and let Canaan be his servant. May God

---

5. Genesis 37:9. John uses the features of both God's curse and Joseph's dream to emphasize that the coming Messiah was being indicated way back in Genesis.

6. E.g., Jeremiah 2:18–25, 33–3:1; Ezekiel 23:1–25; Deuteronomy 28:47–48.

7. The withdrawal of these three blessings is foreseen in the Song of Moses in Deuteronomy 32 (e.g., vv 15–30).

Blight and Blessing in Genesis and Deuteronomy

enlarge Japheth, and let him dwell in the tents of Shem, and let Canaan be his servant.'" (Gen 9:24–27)

So Moses is portraying the blessing on the first man—that he will subdue and have dominion over the animals—as being fulfilled in Shem's offspring subduing and having dominion over Canaan's offspring, and Japheth's offspring (the nations) being drawn to Shem's descendant Israel as per Isaiah 2, just as God brought a remnant of all the animals to Noah and into the ark with him. This curse on Canaan is the true (though not the ultimate) target of God's curse on the serpent in Genesis 3. Isaiah 11 also seems to understand the animals in Genesis as representing nations (again the ESV's "shall" is changed to "will"):

> " . . . with righteousness he will judge the poor, and decide with equity for the meek of the earth; and he will strike the earth with the rod of his mouth, and with the breath of his lips he will slay the wicked. Righteousness will be the belt of his waist, and faithfulness the girdle of his loins. The wolf will sojourn with the lamb, and the leopard will lie down with the young goat,[8] and the calf and the lion and the fattened calf together; and a little child [or simply "boy"] will lead them. The cow and the bear will graze; their young will lie down together; and the lion will eat straw like the ox. The nursing child will play over the hole of the cobra, and the weaned child will put his hand on the adder's den. They will not hurt or destroy in all my holy mountain; for the earth will be full of the knowledge of the LORD as the waters cover the sea.
>
> In that day the root of Jesse, who will stand as a signal for the peoples—of him will the nations inquire, and his resting place will be glorious. The jealousy of Ephraim will depart, and those who harass Judah will be cut off; Ephraim will not be jealous of Judah, and Judah will not harass Ephraim. But they will swoop down on the shoulder of the Philistines in the west, and together they will plunder the people of the east. They will put out their hand against Edom and Moab, and the Ammonites will obey them." (Isa 11:4–14)

In the first paragraph of the above extract, the outcome of the Messiah bringing justice to the weak and the meek is that the carnivores are subdued before the plant-eating livestock. In the second paragraph (which

---

8. Note the reversal here of Deuteronomy 28:43–44, quoted above. The foreign sojourner will no longer subdue or dominate the lambs and goats of God's people, but will be subdued by the child-Messiah, and will come to God's people in order to be with them and be like them, as in Isaiah 2:1–4.

begins the second half of Isaiah 11), the Messiah exercises his lordship over the nations, so that Ephraim's jealousy and Judah's harassment are subdued, and their surrounding nations are also subdued. That is, Isaiah is not talking literally about animals at the end, but is using them to picture the relationship between the Messiah (the "boy"), the people of God (the herbivores), and the nations (the converted carnivores). The repeated portrayal of peaceful relations between young children and snakes is a resolution of the enmity in Genesis 3 between the seed of the woman and the seed of the serpent. The reference to "my holy mountain" completes the picture, as we saw in chapter 1 that Eden is also a mountain.

This means that when Moses refers to God putting the fear of man onto all the animals, he primarily has in mind the fear that even powerful and rapacious rulers (who are thus like top-order carnivores) will have for the godly line of Adam's offspring in Genesis, which from now on will be reckoned through Shem. This is exactly what we see with the next individual in this line, Abraham. Abraham feels vulnerable in the face of the kings of Egypt and Gerar,[9] yet God puts fear into them so that they leave Abraham and his wife well alone,[10] and Abimelech later makes a covenant with Abraham because he is anxious to be at peace with him.[11]

The blessings on Noah's offspring and notably Shem find further fulfillment in Isaac,[12] Jacob,[13] and most importantly, with Israel on the verge of the Promised Land.[14] But the Israelites are afraid of the Anakites who live in Canaan, because they are so big.[15] Therefore a prominent theme in Deuteronomy is that the Anakites are not invincible, and that God will put the fear of Israel into them,[16] as indeed he does,[17] just as he destroyed the Nephilim (usually regarded as giants) in the Flood.[18]

---

9. Genesis 12:10–20; Genesis 20.
10. Genesis 12:20; 20:8, 11.
11. Genesis 21:22–32.
12. Genesis 26:6–16.
13. Genesis 31:29; compare 34:30 with 35:5.
14. Numbers 22:3.
15. Numbers 13:28—14:4; Deuteronomy 1:28.
16. Deuteronomy 2:20—3:11.
17. Joshua 2:9–14.
18. Genesis 6:4.

Blight and Blessing in Genesis and Deuteronomy

This is not to deny that at the literal level this promise of the fear of the animals is still a blessing, and its withdrawal is still a curse.[19] But I think that the animals were made the way they are from the beginning, and that Moses has used some features of the natural world (e.g., man's lordship over the animals, and the natural shyness of most animals toward people) to picture and gradually unfold God's purpose for his children. So these blessings and curses after the Flood are another big step from the original blessing of man's lordship over the animals, towards the covenant blessing of Israel's dominion over the nations in Deuteronomy. So again, the blessings and curses in Genesis are unfolding in a Deuteronomic direction.

The fulfillment of this blessing now is that Jesus has begun to subdue the fearsome and dangerous human rulers before his messengers as they declare his lordship and teach his commandments. Accordingly when Jesus commissioned his disciples he did so with Genesis imagery of carnivores, livestock, "clean" (i.e., innocent) animals, and cunning serpents:

> "I send you out as sheep in the midst of wolves, so be wise as serpents and innocent as doves . . . you will be dragged before governors and kings for my sake, to bear testimony before them and the nations. When they deliver you up, do not be anxious how you are to speak or what you are to say . . . for I will give you a mouth and wisdom which none of your adversaries will be able to withstand . . . not a hair of your head will perish . . . So don't be afraid of them." (Matt 10:16–19, 26; Luke 21:15, 18)

THE RICH LAND OF LONG LIFE

Another parallel between all of humanity in Genesis and Israel in Deuteronomy is that God does not bless his children just anywhere and anyhow: he brings them to a rich land, and dwells there with them, and blesses them through the rich resources around them, with the outcome of long life.[20] This is exactly the story of Israel that Moses teaches them in the following song:

---

19. E.g., Deuteronomy 32:24; 1 Kings 13:21–24; 20:35–36.
20. E.g., Ezekiel 35:10; 48:35. In Psalms 127 and 128 we see these same three blessings of numerous offspring, material prosperity, and (in Psalm 127:3–5) dominion over enemies. In Psalm 133:3 we see the same connection between the dwelling place of God and eternal life.

> "Is he not your father, who created you, who made and established you? ... He found him in a desert land, and in the howling waste of the wilderness ... he ate the produce of the field, and he suckled him with honey out of the rock, and oil out of the flinty rock. Curds from the herd, and milk from the flock, with fat of lambs, rams of Bashan and goats, with the very finest of the wheat—and you drank foaming wine made from the blood of the grape." (Deut 32:6–14)

> "For the LORD your God is bringing you into a good land, a land of brooks of water, and fountains and springs, flowing out in the valleys and hills, a land of wheat and barley, of vines and fig trees and pomegranates, a land of olive trees and honey." (Deut 8:7–8)

> "And when the Lord your God brings you into the land that he swore to your fathers ... and cisterns that you did not dig, and vineyards and olive trees that you did not plant ..." (Deut 6:10–11)

So God uses the well-watered garden land of Canaan as his means of blessing Israel. Accordingly the blessings and curses in Deuteronomy 28 distill to either living long in the land of Canaan, or having life cut short by being driven out of or wiped off the face of the land.[21]

Genesis 2 tells a similar story about the origin of all humanity:

> "When no bush of the open country was yet in the land and no small plant of the open country had yet sprung up—for the LORD God had not caused it to rain on the land, and there was no man to work the ground, and fresh groundwater was going up from the land and was watering the whole face of the ground—then the LORD God formed the man of dust from the ground and breathed into his nostrils the breath of life, and the man became a living creature. And the LORD God planted a garden in Eden, in the east, and there he put the man whom he had formed. And out of the ground the LORD God made to spring up every tree that is pleasant to the sight and good for food. The tree of life was in the midst of the garden, and the tree of the knowledge of good and evil. A river flowed out of Eden to water the garden, and there it divided and became four rivers." (Gen 2:5–10)

---

21. This idea of living long in the land (or not) often surfaces in Deuteronomy, and at key points such as the commandment to honor one's parents (Deut 5:16), the outcome of obeying all the Ten Commandments (Deut 5:33), and Moses' final exhortation to Israel (Deut 30:16–20).

Blight and Blessing in Genesis and Deuteronomy

As in Deuteronomy, God brings the man from "outside" to a well-watered garden land with fruit trees already planted. Outside the garden where the man was created, there seems to be both barren wilderness and irrigated arable land (though the exact relation is uncertain), and this too is like the origins of Israel: while it was in the wilderness that they entered a covenant to become God's children, it was in Egypt that they multiplied.

Eden is also God's chosen place for blessing man in the three areas we noted above. It is in Eden that the man is enabled to have offspring and multiply, because this is where Eve is made,[22] and because Eden is richly fruitful with food from the ground. It is also in Eden that man asserts his dominion over the animals by naming them.[23] Finally, it's in Eden that everlasting life is to be had via the tree of life. So in Genesis 3 when man disobeys and all three blessings are withdrawn, the only physical change we are told of is that man has been driven out from the garden and therefore cut off from eternal life.[24]

Another link between God using Eden to bless man and Canaan to bless Israel is that God also uses Egypt to bless Jacob's family while Joseph is lord there, just as Adam was lord in Eden:

> "Be fruitful and multiply; fill the earth (Heb. 'eretz) and subdue it, and have dominion . . . over every living thing that moves on the earth . . . I have given you every plant yielding seed that is on the face of all the earth, and every tree with seed in its fruit. You shall have them for food. And to . . . everything that has the breath of life, I have given every green plant for food." (Gen 1:28–30)

> "The sons of Israel were fruitful and increased greatly; they multiplied and grew exceedingly strong, so that the land (Heb. 'eretz) was filled with them. Now there arose new king over Egypt, who did not know Joseph. And he said to his people, "Behold, the sons of Israel are too many and too mighty for us." (Exod 1:7–9)

> "Then Joseph settled his father and his brothers and gave them a possession in the land of Egypt, in the best of the land . . . and Joseph provided his father, his brothers, and all his father's household with food . . . And Joseph gathered up all the money that was found in the land of Egypt and in the land of Canaan, in exchange

---

22. Genesis 2:21–22.
23. Genesis 2:18–20.
24. Genesis 3:22–24.

for the grain that they bought . . . So Israel settled in the land of Egypt, in the land of Goshen. And they gained possessions in it, and were fruitful and multiplied greatly." (Gen 47:11–14, 27)

The multiplication of Israel's offspring is the most emphasized parallel with the Genesis 1 blessing, partly because it also relates to the blessing of dominion: it's Israel's sheer numbers that get the later Pharaoh nervous. But it's probably also partly to do with Israel's wealth, which seems to have come about because they were given the best of the land and their grain for free,[25] in contrast to the rest of Egypt and Canaan who had to pay for it. This parallels the third blessing in Genesis 1, namely man's favorable allocation of food relative to the animals.[26] So in Genesis 1 Moses is doing more than just explaining man's position relative to the animals and man's privilege of growing the grain that so many animals covet.

When the lordship of Joseph was finished and forgotten, Egypt ceased to be a place where God could bless Israel. The Pharaoh who "did not know Joseph" responded to Israel's fruitfulness and multiplication by putting them in servitude, killing their sons, and making them work hard for their living.[27] This blighted the three areas in which God wanted to bless Israel, making a move out of Egypt necessary.

But there was another reason why a move out of Egypt was necessary for Israel, just as believers today must leave this world behind.

FORGETTING GOD AMID FRUITFUL GROUND

God did not merely want to materially bless humanity and Israel for the sake of materially blessing them. He wanted them to learn, live out, and love his ways. Material blessing and curse were a carrot and a stick, however much pleasure God has in blessing those who give him pleasure. So a condition of living in the garden is that Adam must refuse to taste and try out his own wisdom of right and wrong, and instead trust and obey God's law. Similarly with Israel: God uses Canaan as his means of blessing obedience

---

25. At first glance, Genesis 47:22 and 26 might indicate that only the priests were allocated grain and didn't have to sell their land. But the point of this part of the narrative seems to be given in verse 27, which is that the Israelites *did* gain possessions and multiply so much in Egypt, relative to the Egyptians. The intentions of Pharaoh and Joseph were that Israel be generously provided for.

26. The grain ("seed") seems to be especially for man rather than the animals.

27. Exodus 1:8–22.

Blight and Blessing in Genesis and Deuteronomy

to his ways, and cursing disobedience by removing them from the land. But as in Eden, Moses foretells in his song that blessing Israel in Canaan won't work for long: "But Jeshurun [Israel] grew fat, and kicked; you grew fat, stout, and sleek; then he forsook God who made him and scoffed at the Rock of his salvation" (Deut 32:15).

Nor does it work after the Flood, when God restores fruitfulness to the ground for righteous Noah:[28]

> "Noah began to be a man of the soil, and he planted a vineyard. He drank of the wine and became drunk and lay uncovered in his tent. And Ham, the father of Canaan, saw the nakedness of his father and told his two brothers outside." (Gen 9:20–22)

So Noah is still "a man of the soil" in that he still has an earthly, soiled nature. The more this soil bears fruit for us, the more corruption it brings out in us as it did for Sodom.[29] Our earthly nature or "flesh" as Paul calls it, needs putting to death rather than feeding abundantly.[30] So we need to be wary of ourselves in the midst of material blessings, and especially of seeking them:[31] they tend to bring out our corruption and choke any longing for righteousness.

Another thing often found with material prosperity is a love of the outward forms of religion such as worship services, when our hearts have turned away somewhat from God's righteousness. This was one of the besetting self-deceptions of Israel,[32] so Moses warns them of it in the example of Cain, whose offerings were unasked for yet whose actions were unrighteous.[33]

So if God must give Israel new hearts, he does it through their painful uprooting and exile from the land:

> "And when all these things come upon you, the blessing and the curse, which I have set before you, and you call them to mind among all the nations where the LORD your God has driven you, and return to the LORD your God, you and your children, and obey his voice in all that I command you today, with all your heart and with all your soul, then the LORD your God will restore your

---

28. Genesis 5:29; 6:9; 8:21.
29. Genesis 8:21; Galatians 6:8; Ezekiel 16:49–50.
30. Romans 8:4–8; 13:14; Colossians 3:5.
31. Mark 4:19; 10:23; 1 Timothy 6:9–10.
32. Isaiah 1:10–15; 58:1–5.
33. Genesis 4:3.

fortunes and have mercy on you, and he will gather you again from the peoples where the LORD your God has scattered you ... And the LORD your God will circumcise your heart and the heart of your offspring, so that you will love the LORD your God with all your heart and with all your soul, that you may live." (Deut 30:1–6)[34]

The hardship of life outside Eden[35] has a similar power to turn hearts back to God, because even in the midst of hardening rebellion against God in Genesis 4, the chapter concludes that "At that time people began to call upon the name of the LORD."[36] But Cain's rebellion only hardened, and so God intensified his curse on the ground for Cain.[37] Likewise God would and did strike Israel harder when they continued to rebel.[38]

For us, it's great to be in a church or Christian community with most of our individual or family's needs met and most things the way we like them. But this often allows persistent areas of idolatry to quietly take over our hearts and church life,[39] so that our love of God's righteousness is gradually replaced by a love of mere "worship," "fellowship," and our own rules and traditions. We say his name more but obey him less, as did Israel.[40] So God has to send trouble into our comfortable environment or, if that is not enough, to uproot us from it, in order to turn our hearts back to him.

God often does this through the reigning earthly powers. He allowed the king of Egypt to take away the blessings of Egypt from Israel, and then allowed Israel to be exiled by and subjected to the king of Babylon.[41] At a more fundamental level God allows the prince of this world, Satan, to take away the blessings of this world from the righteous, as he did with Job.[42] Because our corruption is with us till the day we die, God's people can put away their plans for a prosperous rest from labor in this life, as Job had to do.

---

34. See also Jeremiah 31:33–34; Ezekiel 36:26–27. This is why Jeremiah was appointed "to pull up" (Jer 1:10). Once he had prophesied exile, it would happen.

35. Genesis 3:16–19.

36. Wenham (Gen 1–15, 116) and others regard this verse "as simply noting the beginning of public worship."

37. Genesis 4:11–12.

38. Isaiah 1:5–9.

39. As it was with the persistence and eventual proliferation of high places in Israel.

40. Luke 6:46; Jeremiah 7:4.

41. Jeremiah 27.

42. Job 1–2.

Blight and Blessing in Genesis and Deuteronomy

FROM UNEARNED FAVOR TO ULTIMATE BLESSING

At Bible College we looked a lot at God's grace and how it works out in things like his choosing people and justifying them because of their faith. But I remember an essay question that most people (including me) chose to avoid, the gist of which was, "How does Scripture reconcile God's salvation according to his grace and his judgement according to our works?" We all had Protestant backgrounds that were strong in the area of God's grace, but I think most of us were weaker in our understanding of God's blessing or curse on our conduct and how it relates to God's grace. Pentecostal denominations may place more emphasis on God's blessing, but there is often an emphasis on rather short term and material blessings in contrast to the unfolding and climactic outcome of a person's life that we see in Scripture.

One way that Genesis helps to clarify this relationship between God's works of grace and his blessing on our works, is with its narratives that begin with God's unearned favor to people and culminate with his ultimate blessing on their obedience and ultimate sacrifice. So Noah's life begins with a prophecy from his father at his birth, that "Out of the ground that the LORD has cursed, this one shall bring us rest."[43] The next thing we hear of him is that in contrast with the great corruption and evil intentions of everyone else, "Noah found favor with the LORD."[44] So we see God's grace beginning the story, not Noah's works. But the focus and climax of the story has to do with Noah's obedience and his sacrifice at the end. God similarly favors and sets the agenda for Abraham, Jacob, and Joseph from the beginning, and we have already seen the climactic obedience and sacrifice of some of them. We find the same beginning and climax in Jesus' life:

> "And the child grew and became strong, filled with wisdom. And the favor of God was upon him ... And Jesus increased in wisdom and in stature, and in favor with God and man." (Luke 2:40, 52)

> "Therefore I will divide him a portion with the many, and he shall divide the spoil with the strong, because he poured out his soul to death and was numbered with the transgressors." (Isa 53:12)

> "And being found in human form, he humbled himself by becoming obedient to the extent of death, even death on a cross.

---

43. Genesis 5:29.
44. Genesis 6:7–8.

Therefore God has highly exalted him and bestowed on him the name which is above every name." (Phil 2:8, 9)

"After making purification for sins, he sat down at the right hand of the majesty on high, having become as much superior to angels . . . " (Heb 1:3-4)

So although Paul magnifies God's grace to sinners like himself, his preoccupation is not so much to look back, sit back, and celebrate God's grace,[45] as it is to strain forward to the final reward for his own sacrifice:

"[My goal is] to know him, [which means to know] the power of his resurrection and the fellowship of his sufferings, being continually conformed to his death, if, in some way, I may reach the resurrection from the dead. I do not mean that I have already attained [my ambition] or have already been perfected . . . Just one thing [I focus on]: forgetting what lies behind and straining forward to what lies ahead, I run straight towards the goal in order to win the prize promised by God's heavenly call in Christ Jesus." (Phil 3:10-14)[46]

"For I am already being poured out as a drink offering, and the time for my departure has come. I have fought the good fight, I have finished the race, I have kept the faith. From now on there is laid up for me the crown of righteousness, which the Lord, the righteous judge, will award to me on that day, and not only to me but to all who have longed for his appearing." (2 Tim 4:6-8)

So while our willingness to obey God is the result of his gift and work, his blessing or curse is what we ourselves have earned. This is why even though Paul is outstanding in his time and clearer than most about God's unconditional grace, he knows that his own reward is still not decided as in the Philippians passage above, and as in 1 Corinthians below:

"Every athlete exercises self-control in all things. They do it to receive a perishable wreath, but we an imperishable. So I do not run aimlessly; I do not box as one beating the air. But I beat my body and make it my slave, lest after preaching to others I myself should be disqualified." (1 Cor 9:25-27)

---

45. As in the song "O Happy Day."
46. Translation by O'Brien, *Philippians*, 382, 417.

So there are two errors to avoid. One is to think that if we are rewarded for our works (a clear theme in some of Jesus' parables) then we are taking praise away from God that rightly belongs to him. But God is not only praised for his grace or for his Son, but for the righteousness of all his children:

> "Let your light shine before others, so that they may see your good works and give glory to your Father who is in heaven." (Matt 5:16)

> "Keep your conduct among the nations honorable, so that when they speak against you as evildoers, they may see your good deeds and glorify God on the day of visitation." (1 Pet 2:12)

A second error is to think that God's blessing and curse are relatively prompt responses to individual actions along the way, rather than being his final and permanent response to the final and overall tenor of our lives.[47] This can cause us to be deceived that we are being blessed when our material interests are prospering, and deceived that we are being cursed when they are not:

> "Do not be deceived: God is not mocked, for whatever one sows, that will he also reap. For the one who sows to the flesh will from the flesh reap corruption, but the one who sows to the Spirit will from the Spirit reap eternal life. And let us not grow weary of doing good, for in due season we will reap, if we do not give up." (Gal 6:7–9)

---

47. Few things are more widespread or prominent in Jesus' parables than God's ultimate blessing and curse, and both Isaiah and Revelation end on the same note.

Chapter 7

Ruling the Wicked and Winning the Reward

WHEN I HEAR REPORTS of conflicts abroad, I'm often left ignorant despite all the political (and politically correct) analysis as to what or whom is really driving it. It can be most illuminating sometimes, to hear insider reports that reveal and make sense of what's really going on. It's like this when we read Genesis. We see hostility and rivalry that are often left unexplained, yet occasionally Genesis provides a key to what is really going on, or of what *will* go on. One of these keys is Genesis 3:15, where God says to the serpent, "I will put enmity between you and the woman, and between your offspring and her offspring; he will bash your head, and you will bash his heel" (own translation).

We have already seen that the woman and her offspring point ultimately to Israel and her Messiah who will rule the nations, and also to their anticipations along the way such as Eve and Abel, Rebekah and Jacob, and Rachel and Joseph.[1] So what clues does this sentence provide that help us to rightly understand the conflict and rivalry not only in Genesis, but through the rest of biblical and church history?

---

1. His brothers' jealousy stretches back to the rivalry between Rachel and Leah in Genesis 30:1–15.

Ruling the Wicked and Winning the Reward

BEING WARY OF THE WICKED

One clue that it gives is the reference to serpents. Despite some of the helpful and perceptive dinosaurs in the movie *Jurassic World*,[2] in the real world reptiles have no trust or devotion toward people. Despite what some snake lovers might like to believe, snakes are deaf and blind to any expression of our goodwill or longing for fellowship.[3] They are uncomprehending of our heart and purpose and are better known in the news for tragically turning on people without precedent, or catching them off guard with a lethal bite.[4] So the biblical authors have found snakes to be a fitting image of the wicked in their relationship with God and his people:

> "The wicked are estranged from the womb; they go astray from birth, speaking lies. They have venom like the venom of a serpent, like the deaf adder that stops its ear, so that it does not hear the voice of the charmers . . . " (Ps 58:3–5)[5]

> "To you it has been given to know the secrets of the kingdom of heaven, but to them it has not been given . . . This is why I speak to them in parables, because seeing they do not see, and hearing they do not hear, nor do they understand." (Matt 13:11, 13)

---

2. Many of these dinosaurs display behavior more typically associated with mammals and people.

3. One of my childhood recollections is of a friend telling me how a Dutchman we both knew, brought his Diamond Python to my friend's place, but something went wrong and the end of it was the Dutchman crying "He bite me on de bum! He bite me on de bum!" My wife also tells of a YouTube video in which a young lady took her pet *Boa constrictor* to the vet. Despite the good intentions of the vet and the loving intentions of the owner, both of them end up bitten, with the young lady in tears that her beautiful one could turn against her like that. But I haven't been able to locate the video and provide a link.

4. But Moses is not referring simply to snakes. The Hebrew word here (*naḥash*) also has mythical, symbolic, and dragonish associations as we saw earlier—hence the usual English translation "serpent." The dragonish aspect of this serpent, notably its supreme craftiness and malice toward man (Gen 3:1) parallels the shrewdness and malice of Pharaoh toward Israel in Exodus 1. So Genesis does not endorse a prejudice against all snakes, or killing them all. Even deadly snakes are fine "out there." The problem is when we have to live in close quarters with them, just as the run-ins of the righteous in Genesis are usually with neighbors or family.

5. See also Isaiah 59:1–8.

So Cain's murder of Abel is deceptive and blind to any brotherly ties or guilt.[6] Ham's desire to expose his otherwise outstanding father behind his back is unreasonable compared with Shem's desire to cover his father.[7] And Joseph's brothers "hated him, and could not speak peacefully to him."[8]

So when Joseph sees and yearns for his brothers when they come down to Egypt for grain, he doesn't reveal himself, but rather treats them roughly and tests them.[9] The test proves worthwhile as his brothers are convicted of their guilt,[10] and Judah later rises gloriously to the supreme test.[11]

Even after all of Joseph's kindness toward his brothers, there is little trust or awareness of his heart but only fear of revenge:

> "When Joseph's brothers saw that their father was dead, they said, 'It may be that Joseph will hate us and pay us back for all the evil that we did to him. So they sent a message to Joseph, saying, "Your father gave this command before he died: 'Say to Joseph, "Please forgive the transgression of the servants of the God of your father."' Joseph wept when they spoke to him." (Gen 50:15–17)

The brothers' words indicate that they imagine Joseph's relationship with Jacob has been like their own: a matter of grudging submission while he is around, and disobedience when he is gone (as it was for them when they got rid of Joseph) rather than the love we actually see between Jacob and Joseph. Jesus has likely derived the prodigal son's older brother at least partly from them:[12] "These many years I have slaved for you, and I never disobeyed your command"[13]—yet his heart is far from his father's, however physically close he has stayed.

---

6. Genesis 4:8–9, 13. Cain has no sense that, however hard his punishment, it's less than he deserves.

7. Genesis 9:20–23.

8. Genesis 37:4.

9. Like Joseph, Joab had to be a bit brutal in the face of David's lopsided yearning for Absalom, and David's general lack of wisdom after the civil war (2 Sam 15:13—19:43).

10. Genesis 42:21–24.

11. Genesis 44.

12. Because like the sons of Jacob, the older brother in the parable represents national Israel, while Joseph and Benjamin were the two youngest. Jesus again draws on Joseph's brothers to represent national Israel in the parable of the Tenants, who (as with Joseph's brothers), see the beloved son coming and plot to kill him.

13. Luke 15:29. The NIV's "slaved for you" is more accurate than the ESV's "served you," because the Greek verb in question here—*douleō*—refers to work performed by a slave/bondservant.

Jacob displays a similar yearning yet wariness toward Esau. Although their reconciliation is genuine and heart-warming, Jacob is still wary of Esau because he volunteers that he will go to Seir with him, but he doesn't want Esau or any of Esau's men to travel with him, and then he doesn't go to Seir after all.[14] Edom's later hostility toward Israel when they were returning from Egypt was in some measure a vindication of Jacob's wariness.

Jesus likewise didn't entrust himself to the people when they wanted to make him king, because "he knew what was in man",[15] and had eyes open to the deception of the Jewish leaders and their murderous intent when they seemed to be complimenting him.[16] Jesus teaches his disciples to show the same discernment about the kind of people they are dealing with, even within their own religious family and community:

> "Do not give dogs what is holy, and do not throw your pearls before pigs, lest they trample them underfoot and turn to attack you." (Matt 7:6)

> "Beware of men, for they will deliver you over to courts and flog you in their synagogues . . . Brother will deliver brother over to death, and the father his child, and children will rise against their parents and have them put to death." (Matt 10:17, 21)

So being wary of the wicked is partly for the sake of self-preservation, and partly for the sake of winning a spiritual war, but it does not involve fighting or eliminating people as we will see next.

YET YEARNING FOR OUR KITH AND KIN

The more prominent feature of Joseph's later relationship with his brothers is not his shrewdness but his yearning for them. He keeps on weeping for them.[17] Jeremiah also longed for his eyes to be fountains that could let out

---

14. Genesis 33:12–20.
15. John 2:24–25.
16. John 8:44; Luke 20:20–23.
17. Genesis 42:24; 43:30; 45:1–15; 50:17.

all his sorrow for Israel,[18] Jesus yearned for and wept over Jerusalem,[19] and Paul had "great sorrow and unceasing anguish" for his fellow Israelites.[20]

It might be tempting to think that this yearning for our own flesh and blood comes from the "earthy" part of our nature, but it comes from God himself:

> "Do you not know that friendship with the world is enmity with God? Therefore whoever wishes to be a friend of the world makes himself an enemy of God. Or do you suppose it is to no purpose that the Scripture says, "He yearns jealously over the spirit that he has made to dwell in us?" (Jas 4:4–5)

So our yearning for our own flesh and blood is one of the evidences that the same Spirit dwells in us. Yet this yearning for our own flesh must not lead to ties and obligations that sever our loyalty to God. As we saw in the previous chapter, this is reflected in God's word to Eve that "Your desire will be for your husband, and he will rule over you."[21] Just as Eve would yearn for the man she was formed from, so Israel would yearn for the nations round about that she came from, and intermarry and make treaties with them, and be oppressed by them. But because God's yearning and sorrow are not without fruit, we can have confidence that our own yearning will find some positive response:

> "I ask, then, has God rejected his people? By no means! For I myself am an Israelite, a descendant of Abraham, a member of the tribe of Benjamin ... Inasmuch then as I am an apostle to the Gentiles, I magnify my ministry in order somehow to make my fellow Jews jealous, and thus save some of them." (Rom 11:1, 13–14)

> "That which we have seen and heard we proclaim also to you, so that you too may have fellowship with us; and indeed our fellowship is with the Father and with his Son Jesus Christ. And we are writing these things so that our[22] joy may be complete." (1 John 1:3–4)

---

18. Jeremiah 9:1.
19. Matthew 23:37; Luke 19:41–42.
20. Romans 9:2–3.
21. Genesis 3:16.
22. Some manuscripts have "your joy" but the manuscript support is weaker. The better-attested "our joy" is supported by 2 John 4 & 12, and 3 John 4.

That is, John is confident that his joy will be complete because some of those he is writing to will have fellowship with John in what he is saying, and so with Jesus and the Father also. So the yearning and sorrow of all God's children is that their own flesh and blood are hardened against and uncomprehending of the grace of God toward them, and the goodness of his will. This is why Moses and Jeremiah are reluctant prophets,[23] and why Isaiah and Ezekiel are abundantly forewarned.[24]

So the child of God wants to win hearts rather than arguments, for fellowship rather than for feathers in a cap:

> "The Lord's servant must not be quarrelsome but kind to everyone, able to teach, patiently enduring evil, correcting his opponents with gentleness. God may perhaps grant them repentance leading to a knowledge of the truth, and they may come to their senses and escape from the snare of the devil, after being captured by him to do his will." (2 Tim 2:24–26)

So like Jesus with Judas, God's children may find themselves in close quarters with people who, however they initially appear, have no desire for fellowship with them: no love and no loyalty. But our response is to be one of yearning and sorrow that doesn't give up hope till the end, just as Jesus showed to Judas.[25] Both Jesus and James make clear that wisdom doesn't seek to ruthlessly remove opponents as Solomon did. So Joseph's manifest wisdom coexisted naturally with his yearning and sorrow.

When wisdom loses its yearning for our fellow man, it degenerates into mere rules and knowledge, like the Pharisees of whom Jesus said, "you travel across sea and land to make a single convert, and when he becomes a convert, you make him twice as much a child of hell as yourselves."[26] They only make a single convert because there is no love or relationship in it: only rules to enforce and doctrines to fight for. Jesus, on the other hand, makes disciples who are "fishers of men:" good at winning them.

---

23. Exodus 4:1–13; Jeremiah 1:6.

24. Isaiah 6:8–13; Ezekiel 2:3—3:11.

25. Jesus refused to expose Judas, gave him many opportunities to repent, and grieved at his fate (e.g. Matt 26:24; John 13:21).

26. Matthew 23:15.

AND INNOCENT AS DOVES

> "Behold, I am sending you out as sheep in the midst of wolves, so be wise as serpents, and innocent as doves. Beware of men . . . " (Matt 10:17)

A phenomenon that recurs in the stories of Abraham, Isaac, and Simeon and Levi is that while they are wary toward their powerful neighbors who want their women, they are soundly rebuked for also being deceitful and, with Simeon and Levi, violent and vengeful.[27] Even when Joseph tries to hide from Pharaoh that his brothers are shepherds it backfires awkwardly, so that they end up not only volunteering that they are shepherds but going on to ask Pharaoh if they can live in the best part of the land![28]

WINNING BY WITNESS BUT LOSING OUR LIVES

God's curse on the serpent that the woman's offspring "will bash your head, and you will bash his heel," indicates some harm to God's people, and this is confirmed in the next chapter of Genesis when Cain murders Abel. In fact it seems as if Abel is the one with the bashed head, while Cain comes off more lightly. Yet in a sense Abel has won, in that Cain has not been able to silence the blood which proclaims his own guilt: "And the LORD said, 'What have you done? Your brother's blood is crying to me from the ground'" (Gen 4:10).

This inability of Satan and his offspring to silence the witness of God's people continues through the prophets to Jesus' disciples:

> "They will lay their hands on you and persecute you, delivering you up to the synagogues and prisons, and you will be brought before kings and governors . . . I will give you a mouth and wisdom, which none of your adversaries will be able to withstand or contradict." (Luke 21:12, 15)

Even in our righteous living, witness is borne to God's righteousness:

> "Do all things without grumbling or disputing, that you may be blameless and innocent, children of God without blemish in the midst of a crooked and twisted generation, among whom you

---

27. Genesis 12:10–20; 20:1–13; 26:6–11; 34:13–30; 49:5–7.
28. Genesis 46:31—47:4.

Ruling the Wicked and Winning the Reward

shine as lights in the world, holding fast to the word of life" (Phil 2:14–16).

However, it's not our witness to God as such that defeats Satan. It's not merely a matter of cause and effect, but is a blessing given by God:

> "[Jesus] said to them, 'But who do you say that I am?' Simon Peter replied, 'You are the Christ, the son of the living God.' And Jesus answered him, 'Blessed are you, Simon bar-Jonah. For flesh and blood has not revealed this to you, but my Father in heaven. And I tell you, you are Peter, and on this rock [Greek *petra*] I will build my church, and the gates of hell will not prevail against it. I will give you the keys of the kingdom of heaven, and whatever you bind on earth will be bound in heaven, and whatever you release on earth will be released in heaven.'" (Matt 16:16–19)

While death might seem like defeat, it is in a sense the ultimate victory, because it testifies forever and more powerfully than anything else, that one's persecutors are wicked, and that God's salvation and judgement are sure enough to die for:

> "And the great dragon was thrown down, that ancient serpent, who is called the devil and Satan, the deceiver of the whole world ... And they have conquered him by the blood of the lamb and by the word of their testimony, for they loved not their lives even unto death." (Rev 12:9, 11)

> "And he seized the dragon, that ancient serpent, who is the devil and Satan, and bound him for a thousand years, and threw him into the pit, and shut it and sealed it over him, so that he might not deceive the nations any longer, until the thousand years were ended ... Also I saw the souls of those who had been beheaded for the testimony of Jesus and for the word of God ... They came to life and reigned with Christ a thousand years." (Rev 20:2–4)

This second passage is about the influence that God's murdered witnesses will continue to have down through history. It's not talking about the final resurrection, which is the second and ultimate reason why losing one's life for witnessing to God will be the ultimate victory, because it will win the ultimate reward. So now we turn to this final subject of winning God's reward.

PERSONAL SACRIFICE AND PLEADING FOR SINNERS

Until recently I thought that Noah's burnt offerings after the Flood were merely an expression of thanks and "worship." But a comparison with Moses' intercession for Israel indicates otherwise. One of Moses' most shining moments was after the Golden Calf incident, where he laid aside his own life and his own interests to plead and make atonement for Israel when they were at their worst:

> "And the LORD said to Moses, 'I have seen this people, and behold, it is a stiff-necked people. Now therefore let me alone, that my wrath may burn hot against them and I may consume them, in order that I may make a great nation of you.' But Moses implored the LORD his God and said, '. . . Turn from your burning anger and relent from this disaster against your people . . . if you will forgive their sin—but if not, please blot me out of your book that you have written.' (Exod 32:9–12, 32)

> "Now therefore, if I have found favor in your sight, please show me now your ways, that I may know you in order to find favor in your sight. Consider too that this nation is your people.' And he said, 'My presence will go with you, and will give you rest' [just as Lamech prophesied that rest would come through his son Noah]. And he said to him, 'If your presence will not go with me, do not bring us up from here. For how shall it be known that I have found favor in your sight, I and your people? Is it not in your going out with us, so that we are distinct, I and your people, from every other people on the face of the earth?' And the LORD said to Moses, 'This very thing that you have spoken I will do for you, for you have found favor in my sight, and I know you by name.'" (Exod 33:13–17)

> "And he said, 'Behold, I am making a covenant. Before all your people I will do marvels, such as have not been created in all the earth or in any nation. And all the people among whom you are shall see the work of the LORD, for it is an awesome thing that I will do with you.'" (Exod 34:10) [29]

So although God has blessed Israel and given them his law, they have broken it. But Moses sacrifices his own interests for the sake of a sinful and stubborn people. He pleads for them and seeks to atone for their sin. In

---

29. The two "you's" in this sentence are both singular.

consequence, God (who has not yet sworn an oath confirming the Sinai covenant) makes a new covenant with Moses which is not directly with Israel, but is with them over Moses' shoulder, so to speak.

It's like the sequence of events in early Genesis where God blesses man and gives him his law, but man breaks it and degenerates to his worst just before the Flood. But Noah finds favor with God, who shows Noah all his requirements for the ark and then makes a covenant that is with all of life, but through Noah and because of Noah's sacrifice after the Flood:

> "Then Noah built an altar to the Lord and took some of every clean animal and some of every clean bird and offered burnt offerings on the altar. And when the Lord smelled the pleasing aroma, the Lord said in his heart, 'I will never again curse the ground because of man, for the intention of man's heart is evil from his youth. Neither will I ever again strike down every living creature as I have done.'" (Gen 8:20–21)

> "Then God said to Noah and to his sons with him, 'Behold, I establish my covenant with you and your offspring after you, and with every creature that is with you, the birds, the livestock, and every beast of the earth with you, as many as came out of the ark; it is for every beast of the earth.'" (Gen 9:8–10)

What this all indicates to me is that God is not responding arbitrarily to Noah's sacrifice and saying, "That smells nice, I think I'll make a covenant." Rather, God is responding to Noah's burnt offerings because they are intended as a kind of atonement and intercession for all people and animals, as Moses did for Israel. One can imagine that these issues were on Noah's mind after the Flood: "How long before we all become wicked again and God blots us all out again? What has been the point of it all?" And like Moses' plea for Israel it involved personal cost for Noah, as he was giving up some of his precious livestock.[30]

We see a similar situation with Abraham. Out of the blue, God promises to bless him with offspring etc.[31] Then God gives Abraham his requirements of being blameless and circumcising his male offspring and his household, and Abraham intercedes for Lot and his family when God is

---

30. According to Leviticus 11, the clean animals included sheep, cattle, goats, pigeons, and doves, as in Abraham's sacrifice in Genesis 15:9.
31. Genesis 12.

about to destroy Sodom.[32] Finally Abraham virtually sacrifices Isaac, which moves God to swear an oath confirming all his covenant promises.[33]

So Genesis is driving home the point that the thing God really rewards is personal sacrifice, especially in pleading for sinners. This is why a priesthood offering sacrifices for the people was the heart of Israel's formal religion, and its fulfillment in Jesus was in the same categories of atonement, sacrifice, and intercession:

> "When you make his life an offering for sin, he will see his offspring; he will prolong his days . . . by knowledge of him, the righteous one—my servant—will make many to be accounted righteous . . . because he poured out his life to death . . . he bore the sin of many, and made intercession for the transgressors." (Isa 53:10–12)

But we see here and in Genesis that God really wants this sacrifice and intercession at the individual, personal, relational level rather than the formal, symbolic level. This is evident in other figures from Genesis and in Scripture more generally. For example, the thing that made the difference between the offerings of Cain and Abel was that Abel offered his first and best, while Cain's offering was nondescript.[34] Joseph speaks up for the sake of his father's flock although he knows it will make his brothers hate him more, and then he obediently goes out to check on his brothers when he knows he will meet them far from the safety of home.[35] Judah pleads with Joseph to allow himself to remain as Joseph's slave rather than Benjamin, for the sake of their father.[36] It is these actions that bring on Jacob's powerful blessing of Joseph and Judah, and therefore the blessing of God himself.[37]

---

32. Genesis 18.

33. Genesis 22.

34. Wenham, *Genesis 1–15*, 104.

35. Genesis 37:2, 12–16. The parallel between Abraham obediently sacrificing Isaac and Joseph obediently sacrificing himself for Jacob, is underlined by both Abraham and Joseph responding with "Here I am," three times for Abraham (Gen 22:1, 7, 11).

36. Genesis 44.

37. In Genesis there is a transition from God blessing and cursing people directly in the beginning, to God blessing or cursing people through the blessing or curse of Abraham's offspring (Isaac and Jacob), just as God had promised (Gen 12:3; 22:18). This is paralleled in the gospels by Jesus initially pronouncing blessings and woes himself, but then telling his disciples that after he had gone, his blessing and curse would now be determined by and mediated through themselves (Matt 18:18–20; John 20:23).

The story is similar with David. Other people might use God to climb to the top and then when they have "made it," God gets abandoned and forgotten. But when David gets to the "top" he senses the incongruity of his own beautiful palace compared to the tent of the God who gave him all his honor and success.[38] David wants God to get the glory rather than himself, and this moves God to swear his covenant oath of an everlasting heir for David.[39]

At the end of David's reign when the plague comes upon Israel via a destroying angel, David intercedes for Israel and is directed to go up and offer sacrifices on the threshing floor of Araunah the Jebusite (i.e., a native Canaanite and therefore possibly a second-class citizen). In fear at seeing the destroying angel pause over his threshing floor, Araunah offers all his threshing hardware including cattle for free. David responds,

> "'No, but I will buy it from you for a price. I will not offer burnt offerings to the LORD that cost me nothing.' So David bought the threshing floor and the oxen for fifty shekels of silver. And David built there an altar to the LORD and offered burnt offerings and peace offerings. So the LORD responded to the plea for the land, and the plague was averted from Israel." (2 Sam 24:24–25)

So we see this same personal sacrifice and pleading for sinners with David, and how God rewards it. This is the true worship that was at the heart of Israelite religion and of Jesus, because it is the only way to show true love: unmerited, and at personal cost. So when our notions of worship become dominated by emotionally charged or civilized and eloquent gatherings with like-minded others, we need to remember that the love and worship God really wants may be much more wrenching and solitary than we want, as Abraham and Jesus found on (or near) Mount Moriah: "My God, my God, why have you forsaken me?" (Matt 27:46).

This love and worship also involves living with and pleading for neighbors and family who are as hard for us to bear as they were for Moses and Jesus when they came down from fellowship with God on other mountains:

> "And as soon as he came near the camp and saw the calf and the dancing, Moses' anger burned hot, and he threw the tablets out of his hands and broke them at the foot of the mountain." (Exod 32:19)

---

38. 2 Samuel 7:1–2.
39. 2 Samuel 7:12–16.

"O faithless generation, how long am I to be with you? How long am I to bear with you?" (Mark 9:19)

SEEING THE OFFSPRING OF OUR SOLITUDE AND SORROW[40]

We have seen that Genesis ends with the fulfillment of much of its beginning. Joseph is the more righteous and glorious image of God than Adam. In fulfillment of God's blessing on man, Israel has been fruitful and multiplied in the rich land of Goshen, Joseph has glory and dominion in Egypt, and he has subdued his unruly and sometimes ferocious brothers. Finally, Joseph has at last been re-united with his own flesh just as Adam was re-united to his own flesh in his wife.

But unlike the very end of Scripture and of this world,[41] we have seen that there is still weeping at the end of Genesis. Joseph is still a fairly solitary figure, feared and mistrusted rather than loved and known by his brothers. His mother Rachel has died early and in sorrow, leaving him just one full brother, and his father Jacob can only find fellowship and encouragement in two of his twelve sons. So in the book of Isaiah, God's ultimate reward for the righteous remnant of Israel is that they will at last see and be with all their true brothers and children before God, with nothing to spoil their fellowship anymore.[42]

This might seem to conflict with Jesus' promise that "there is no one who has left house or wife or brothers or parents *or children*, for the sake of the kingdom of God, who will not receive many times more *in this time*, and in the age to come eternal life" (Luke 18:29–30). But Genesis distinguishes between God's general blessing that Abraham will father many nations and kings in this age, and God's particular blessing of many offspring *who walk in the footsteps of his faith*, which is fulfilled through Isaac rather than Ishmael and Jacob rather than Esau, and ultimately through Christ.

Jesus was similarly blessed with many followers in this life who ultimately turned away. His true blessing is everlasting fellowship with and glory from those who are made holy and faithful to the end, which Jesus hasn't yet seen. So those who make this sacrifice of leaving homes and

---

40. Genesis 35:18; compare Jeremiah 31:15–17.
41. Revelation 21:4.
42. Isaiah 49:18–22; 53:10; 60:4–22; 65:17–23; 66:7–24.

children will indeed be rewarded with abundant children (whether or not they are biological) who will indeed be a blessing in this life. But many—perhaps even most of them—will not be in God's crowning blessing on our sacrifice and labor.

So the crown of righteousness that Paul spoke of earlier seems to be especially that he will see all his spiritual children—who are his brothers and sisters—perfected and presented to Christ *at the end*:

> "For what is our hope or joy or crown of boasting before our Lord Jesus at his coming? Is it not you? For you are our glory and joy." (1 Thess 2:19-20)

> "... that we may present everyone mature in Christ. For this I toil, struggling [Greek *agōnizomai*] with all his energy that he powerfully works within me." (Col 1:28-29)

The Greek word above for "struggling" also contains nuances of anguish and anxiety,[43] and in Isaiah also these children of Judah and Jerusalem are the fruit of the suffering of Israel's righteous remnant, particularly in their exile.[44] These children are not ethnic Israelites but Gentiles from all the nations, and they are born abruptly:

> "The children of your bereavement will yet say in your ears: 'The place is too narrow for me; make room for me to dwell in.' Then you will say in your heart, 'Who has borne me these? I was bereaved and barren, exiled and put away, but who has brought up these? Behold, I was left alone; from where have these come?'
>
> Thus says the Lord God: 'Behold, I will lift up my hand to the nations, and raise my signal to the peoples; and they shall bring your sons in their arms, and your daughters shall be carried on their shoulders.'" (Isa 49:20-22)

> "And the foreigners who join themselves to the Lord, to minister to him, to love the name of the Lord, and to be his servants ... these I will bring to my holy mountain, and make them joyful in my house of prayer: their burnt offerings and their sacrifices will be accepted on my altar ... The Lord God, who gathers the

---

43. See *agōnizomai* and related (cognate) words in BAGD, 15.

44. Though Isaiah has made clear that at a deeper level they will only come through the suffering of the Servant Messiah.

outcasts of Israel, declares, 'I will gather yet others to him, besides those already gathered.'" (Isa 56:6–8)

"Shall a nation be brought forth in one moment? For as soon as Zion was in labor she brought forth her children . . . I will send [ethnic Jewish] survivors to the nations, to Tarshish, Pul, and Lud, who draw the bow, to Tubal and Javan, to the coastlands far away, that have not heard my fame or seen my glory. And they shall declare my glory among the nations. And they shall bring all your brothers from all the nations as an offering to the Lord, on horses and in chariots and in litters and on mules and on dromedaries, to my holy mountain Jerusalem." (Isa 66:8, 19–20)

The book of Revelation portrays a similar picture: the 144, 000 who are sealed from the twelve tribes of Israel have grown abruptly into "a great multitude that no one could number, from every nation, from all tribes and peoples and languages, standing before the throne and before the Lamb, clothed in white robes."[45] Again they are the fruit of suffering: "Then one of the elders addressed me, saying, 'Who are these, clothed in white robes, and from where have they come?' . . . 'These are the ones coming out of the great tribulation'" (Rev 7:13–14).

In contrast to this vast gathering for worship and fellowship, Genesis and Scripture generally portray a more solitary walk with God through this life. It's true that the men of God in Genesis all had wives, and probably enjoyed a measure of other family fellowship, perhaps between Noah and Shem, Abraham and Isaac, Rebekah and Jacob, and Judah and Joseph. But overall we don't see much happening between or even within families.

Later on, even in the midst of the multitudes of Israelites, priests, and prophets, God's people were often alone,[46] and Adam's waiting and longing for someone like himself is a foreshadowing both of this, and of Jesus' waiting till God has finished building and preparing his bride the church.[47] Likewise at the beginning of Paul's ministry he did not meet with the other apostles in Jerusalem for three years,[48] and even after that he hardly saw them. At the end of his ministry he said to Timothy, "You are aware that all

---

45. Revelation 7:4–9.
46. 1 Kings 19:13–14; Psalms 25:16; 38:11; 69:8; Jeremiah 9:4; 12:6; 15:10; Micah 7:2, 5.
47. Revelation 19:7–8; 21:2.
48. Galatians 1:15–18.

who are in Asia turned away from me . . . At my first defense no one came to stand by me."[49]

So while there are times and occasions of fellowship and encouragement, there are also times when God's people are isolated even within established churches, and where their words are not wanted by those in power. But then God provides fellowship and exhortation in unlikely people and places,[50] as with Melchizedek, Jethro, Ruth, and the Magi. Jesus pointed out and experienced the same reality:

> "And he came to Nazareth, where he had been brought up. And as was his custom, he went to the synagogue on the Sabbath day, and he stood up to read . . . And he said, 'Truly, I tell you, no prophet is acceptable in his home town . . . There were many widows in Israel in the days of Elijah, when the heavens were shut up three years and six months, and a great famine came over all the land, and Elijah was sent to none of them but only to Zarephath, in the land of Sidon, to a woman who was a widow . . .' When they heard these things, all in the synagogue were filled with wrath. And they rose up and drove him out of the town . . . " (Luke 4:16, 24–29)

> "When the centurion heard about Jesus, he sent to him elders of the Jews, asking him to come and heal his servant. And when they came to Jesus, they pleaded with him earnestly, saying, 'He is worthy to have you do this for him, for he loves our nation, and he is the one who built us our synagogue. And Jesus went with them. When he was not far from the house, the centurion sent friends, saying, 'Lord, do not trouble yourself, for I am not worthy to have you come under my roof. Therefore I did not presume to come to you. But say the word, and let my servant be healed . . . When Jesus heard these things, he marveled at him, and turning to the crowd that followed him, said, 'I tell you, not even in Israel have I found such faith.'" (Luke 7:9)

So Jesus—who doesn't share their love of privileges and places in this life—is perhaps rated less highly by them than the man of standing in the community who built them their synagogue. Jesus found more faith on the fringes and more fellowship with figures from the past like Moses and Elijah,[51] than in the synagogues that were the center of Jewish religious life.

49. 2 Timothy 1:15; 4:16.
50. This is a key part of Tolkien's thinking about fellowship. One place where it surfaces is in Elrond's counsel to Frodo in Rivendell (Tolkien, *Fellowship of the Ring*, 288).
51. Mark 9:4.

In contrast to the Jews who could point to their synagogues and temple, and the church congregations with their buildings and benefactors, God's people "have not come to what may be touched . . . But you have come to Mount Zion and to the city of the living God, the heavenly Jerusalem, and to innumerable saints in festal gathering, and to the assembly of the firstborn who are enrolled in heaven."[52] We are already "surrounded by so great a cloud of witnesses" who have gone before us and urge us on by their example.[53]

So our ultimate reward is not something to try and make solid and visible in this life. We are not to settle down here and seek honor and surround ourselves with personal disciples and cozy Christian community, but like Abraham we are to look forward confidently to when God will do this.[54]

While we very much need "to stir up one another to love and good works, not neglecting to meet together,"[55] this unfortunately does not equate with many church services and their aftermath, where there are often too many empty and increasingly unbearable words, and too little of the real interchange that really strengthens and grows our love and good lives. We are not required to attend or prop up such places, which only burden and discourage us and our children. Whoever else may still be doggedly attending, Jesus is not there anymore, but has been driven out by the same unbearable worship that God hated in Isaiah 1, and which caused him to leave the temple in Ezekiel 10.

If we want to be with Jesus and his life-giving presence we must "go to him outside the camp and bear the reproach he endured."[56] This is where we will be encouraged by unexpected fellowship as Abraham was when Melchizedek met him and the angels ate with him. This is where we will be given spiritual children in the midst of our sorrows even if we don't yet know it, or don't yet get to see and enjoy the final outcome of their faith.

---

52. Hebrews 12:18, 22–23.
53. Hebrews 12:1.
54. Hebrews 11:10.
55. Hebrews 10:24–25.
56. Hebrews 13:13.

Bibliography

Alexander, T. D. *From Paradise to the Promised Land*, 2nd ed. Paternoster: Carlisle; Baker: Grand Rapids, 2002.
Assyrian International News Agency. "The Epic of Gilgamesh." Books Online. Downloaded February 14, 2016. http://www.aina.org/books/eog/eog.pdf
Atkinson, David. *The Message of Genesis* 1–11. BST. Leicester, IVP, 1990.
Augustine. *St Augustine: The Literal Meaning of Genesis, Vol.* 1. Translated and annotated by John Hammond Taylor. ACW 41. Mahwah NJ: Paulist, 1982.
Baugher, Cory. "Yahweh's Conflict with the Leviathan and the Sea." 2007. *knowingthebible. net*. Accessed February 1, 2016. http://www.knowingthebible.net/yahweh-the-leviathan-and-sea
Baumgardner, John R., and Jeremy D. Lyon. "A Linguistic Argument for God's Existence." *JETS* 58/4 (2015) 771–786.
Bauer, Walter, W.F. Arndt, F.W. Gingrich and Frederick W. Danker. *A Greek-English Lexicon of the New Testament and other Early Christian Literature*, 2nd ed. Chicago: University of Chicago Press, 1979.
Biblical Training Institute Library, "Daughter of Zion," accessed December 9, 2016. https://www.biblicaltraining.org/library/daughter-zion
Blocher, Henri. *In the Beginning*. Leicester: IVP, 1984.
Byrne, Charles. *Dear Brothers and Sisters*. Mark Ingram, 2016.
Calvin, John. *Institutes of the Christian Religion Vol.* 2. LCC XXI. Translated by Ford Lewis Battles. Edited by John T. McNeill. Philadelphia: Westminster, 1960.
Chadwick, Owen. *The Reformation*. London: Penguin, 1964
Cole, R. Alan. *Exodus*. TOTC. Leicester: IVP, 1973.
Davids, Peter H. "What Glasses are you Wearing? Reading Hebrew Narratives through Second Temple Lenses." *JETS* 55/4 (2012) 763–771.
Doyle, Arthur Conan. *Sherlock Holmes: The Adventures & Memoirs*. Leicester: Galley, 1988.
Espak, Peeter. *The God Enki in Sumerian Royal Ideology and Mythology*. Dissertationes Theologiae Universitatis Tartuensis 19. Tartu: Tartu University Press, 2010.

Bibliography

Faulkner, Danny R., and Don B. DeYoung. "Toward a Creationist Astronomy." *CRS Quarterly* 28/3 (1991). http://www.creationresearch.org/crsq/articles/28/28_3/starevol.html

Foster & Smith, Drs, Educational Staff. "Respiratory System of Birds: Anatomy and Function." Accessed 22nd of May, 2016. http://www.peteducation.com/article.cfm?c=15+1829&aid=2721

Fukuoka, Masanobu. *The One Straw Revolution*. New York: NYRB Classics, 2009.

Heyman, David (Producer) and Chris Columbus (Director), *Harry Potter and the Philosopher's Stone* [Motion Picture]. USA: Warner Bros, 2001.

Hewitt, Raymond. "Creation Myths." *usbible.com*. Accessed February 1, 2016. http://www.usbible.com/Creation/creation_myths.htm

Holladay, W. L. (ed.). *A Concise Hebrew and Aramaic Lexicon of the Old Testament*. Leiden: E. J. Brill, 1988.

Jeanson, Nathaniel T. "Did Lions Roam the Garden of Eden?" *Acts & Facts* 42/7 (2013) 13. https://www.icr.org/article/7534

Kidner, Derek. *Psalms 73–150*. TOTC. Leicester: IVP, 1975.

Kovacs, Maureen Gallery, and Wolf Carnahan. "The Epic of Gilgamesh." 1998. Accessed February 16, 2016. http://www.ancienttexts.org/library/mesopotamian/gilgamesh

Kramer, Samuel Noah, and John R. Maier. *Myths of Enki, the Crafty God*. Oxford: Oxford University Press, 1989.

Lam, Joseph. "The Biblical Creation in its Ancient Near Eastern Context." *biologos.org*. Accessed February 1, 2016. http://biologos.org/uploads/projects/lam_scholarly_essay.pdf.

Lambert, W. G. *Babylonian Wisdom Literature* 2nd ed. Winona Lake: Eisenbrauns, 1996.

Law, Henry. *The Gospel in Genesis*. Edinburgh: Banner of Truth, 1960.

Lin, Grace. *Where the Mountain Meets the Moon*. New York: Little, Brown and Co., 2009.

Lundbom, Jack R. *Jeremiah 1–20*. New Haven: Yale University, 1999.

Matson, Dave E. "How Good Are Those Young-Earth Arguments?" 1994–2002, para. 21. Accessed May 4, 2016. http://www.talkorigins.org/faqs/hovind/howgood-yea2.html

O'Brien, Peter T. *The Epistle to the Philippians*. Grand Rapids: Eerdmans; Carlisle: Paternoster, 1991.

Pipa, Joseph A. "From Chaos to Cosmos: A Critique of the Framework Hypothesis." 1998. Accessed February 1, 2016. www.westminsterreformedchurch.org/ScienceMTS/Science.Pipa.Framework.Critique.htm.

Reid, Andrew. *Salvation Begins: Reading Genesis Today*. Sydney: Aquila, 2000.

Ronning, John. "Creation or Redemption: When Did God Defeat Rahab/Leviathan?" Paper Presented at 2013 Annual ETS Convention, 2013. https://www.academia.edu/7783524/Creation_or_Redemption_When_Did_God_Defeat_Rahab_Leviathan

Rozefelds, A. C. "*Eucalyptus* phylogeny and history: a brief summary." *Tasforests* Vol. 8 (1996) 15–26. Accessed May 4, 2016. https://cdn.forestrytasmania.com.au/assets/0000/0377/vol_8_pages15-26.pdf

Salem, Sema'an I., and Lynda A. Salem. *The Near East, the Cradle of Western Civilization*. Lincoln: Writers Club, 2000.

Seow, C. L. *A Grammar for Biblical Hebrew*, Rev. ed. Nashville: Abingdon, 1995.

Tolkien, J. R. R. *The Fellowship of the Ring*. London: Allen & Unwin, 1954.

———. *The Hobbit*. London: Allen & Unwin, 1978.

———. *The Two Towers*. Boston: Houghton Mifflin, 1954.

Bibliography

Waltke, Bruce K., and M. O'Connor. *An Introduction to Biblical Hebrew Syntax*. Winona Lake: Eisenbrauns, 1990.

Wenham, Gordon J. *Genesis 1–15*. Waco: Word, 1987.

———. *Genesis 16–50*. Dallas: Word, 1994.

Wikipedia. "Abzu." Accessed December 31, 2016. https://en.wikipedia.org/wiki/Abzu

———. "Atra-Hasis." Accessed May 15, 2016. https://en.wikipedia.org/wiki/Atra-Hasis.

———. "Charles Manson." Accessed September 27, 2016. https://en.wikipedia.org/wiki/Charles_Manson

———. "Epic of Gilgamesh." Accessed February 16, 2016. https://en.wikipedia.org/wiki/Epic_of_Gilgamesh;

———. "Garden of the Gods (Sumerian Paradise)." Accessed February 16, 2016. https://en.wikipedia.org/wiki/Garden_of_the_gods_(Sumerian_paradise)

———. "Instruction of Amenemope." Accessed September 11, 2016. https://en.wikipedia.org/wiki/Instruction_of_Amenemope

Wood, Todd Charles. "Mediated Design." *Acts & Facts* 32/9 (2003). http://www.icr.org/article/mediated-design/

Yeo, John. "The Inerrancy and Historicity of Genesis 1–3, Part 2". Last modified January 13, 2014. http://theologicalmatters.com/2014/01/13/the-inerrancy-and-historicity-of-genesis-1-3-part-2/

www.ingramcontent.com/pod-product-compliance
Lightning Source LLC
Chambersburg PA
CBHW050831160426
43192CB00010B/1983